THE DRAWINGS OF
MORRIS GRAVES

BIRD OF PREY 1957
Sumi ink on paper,
34 x 22¾ inches
The Minnesota Museum of Art,
St. Paul

THE DRAWINGS OF
MORRIS GRAVES

WITH COMMENTS BY THE ARTIST

JOHN CAGE, SERIES RE MORRIS GRAVES

DAVID DANIELS, PREFACE

EDITED BY IDA E. RUBIN

PUBLISHED FOR THE DRAWING SOCIETY, INC.

BY NEW YORK GRAPHIC SOCIETY, BOSTON

Previous books in this series by The Drawing Society were: *The Drawings of Edwin Dickinson* by Lloyd Goodrich (Yale University Press, New Haven); *The Drawings of Charles Burchfield* edited by Edith H. Jones (Frederick A. Praeger Publishers, New York); and *Jackson Pollock: Works on Paper* by Bernice Rose (The Museum of Modern Art, New York).

International Standard Book Number 0-316-19305-4
Library of Congress Catalog Card Number 73–89952

Copyright © 1974 by The Drawing Society, Inc.
41 E. 65th St., New York, N.Y. 10021
"Series re Morris Graves" copyright © 1974 by John Cage.
First published 1974 by New York Graphic Society Ltd.
11 Beacon St., Boston, Mass. 02108
First printing 1974

Manufactured in the United States of America

PHOTOGRAPH CREDITS

Oliver Baker, New York: 95, 97, 99, 117; Geoffrey Clements, New York: Frontispiece, 6, 43, 51, 69, 87, 91, 101, 103, 105, 109, 111, 113, 119, 129, 131, 133, 135, 137, 139, 141, 143, 145, 149; Jonas Dovydenas, Chicago: 125; Paulus Leeser, New York: 121; Patricia Magruder, Dallas: 127; Edward Peterson, New York: 123; Sanborn Studio, Wilmington: 93; Gerald Stableski, New York: 45; Adolph Studly, New York: 75, 85; Frank J. Thomas, Los Angeles: 115; Charles Uht, New York: 71, 77, 79, 147.

CONTENTS

GANDERS   1955
Pencil on paper, 30 x 40 inches
Collection Dr. Alvin Friedman-Kein,
New York

PREFACE

The Drawings of Morris Graves marks The Drawing Society's fourth monograph devoted to the drawings of an American artist. The question immediately arises as to why so little has been published on the graphic work of this poetic and prophetic artist, Morris Graves. Was it perhaps because the bombastic thunderings of the New York School and the brittle chic of Pop and Op had temporarily drowned out a clear, gentle voice not demanding attention? Perhaps. Also perhaps, it took time for many to understand that Graves' works, often viewed merely as bird pictures, had a meaning and a beauty that went far deeper, as the artist's statements in this book reveal.

Morris Graves' pictures are included in museums and private collections across the United States, but anyone seriously interested in understanding his work will want to see The Morris Graves Archival Collection at the Museum of Art of the University of Oregon in Eugene. This remarkable group of 490 studies, drawings, and paintings—covering a period of thirty years—was given to the Museum in 1967 by the artist and Mr. Rolf Klep.

When we decided to do this book, Mr. Graves came East to discuss the project. This was the beginning of a fascinating collaboration with the artist, who participated in the selection of the works to be included and also provided perceptive comments on the drawings themselves. Various conversations with the artist were taped at the home of Mr. Graves' longtime friend and dealer, Marian Willard Johnson. Others present were Ida E. Rubin, the dedicated editor of this book, Nancy Wilson Ross, another close friend of the artist, and myself.

Many things that emerged were immensely instructive, even eye-opening. For example, we perceived such drawings as the "Nightfall Pieces" and "Scream Laughter Cup" as the vehement anti-war protests they were. Of the latter, Mr. Graves says, "The Second World War was declared. . . . How could you gasp out a comment that really ended in a shriek, and have it imply multiple fangs?" We saw that Graves was a serious ecologist long before the word was popularized; countless drawings are anguished cries against the pollution of our land, our water, our air.

And what of the birds that appear so often in Morris Graves' work? The bird, usually alone, a symbol of solitude, tries over and over "to satisfy this need for a more deeply integrated environment." The bird: solitary, guarded, disoriented in an environment gone mad. It is no accident that Graves calls many of these bird and animal drawings "self-portraits."

Morris Graves' comments appear opposite the specific drawings, but he felt that some of his drawings needed no comment—a refreshing attitude in today's world of verbose artists. The statement had, after all, been made and was there for

YAK 1936
Pencil on paper, 10½ x 13½ inches
Collection Mr. and Mrs. Jay Goldberg,
Aberdeen, Washington

the viewer to interpret. As in the theatre, the artist offers us "selected reality," the reality of his unique way of seeing life.

The technique of the hand that holds the brush is important only as a means to the end of showing us things, both physical and spiritual, that his genius and vision have perceived in the object. A great artist shows us not the world as it really is, but re-interprets it for us through his own inner eye and spirit.

It is this "inner eye" in Morris Graves' work that is perhaps the most fascinating and seductive thing about it. The line is incredibly delicate and sure at the same time, and yet it never overwhelms us by its virtuosity, nor does it harangue us. Rather the artist suggests possibilities, esthetic as well as spiritual. He gently offers us his subtle, spiritual images, and then vanishes, leaving us to contemplate, to wonder and be moved.

"Spiritual" is a difficult word to avoid in discussing either Morris Graves or his work. He is, in the real sense of the word, a religious artist, and his disenchantment with his family's church, which he found "a church barren in beauty," led him to Zen Buddhism, with its stress on the meditative, to Taoism, and East Indian religion and thought, then back to Christianity. (He did, however, destroy the large body of work he did at Chartres—the old religious symbols simply did not work for him.) He was evolving his own personal symbols, not lost symbols, but symbols of a new religion in which he was high priest in a church without walls.

In his search for spiritual values and in his concern for the environment, Graves parallels so closely the feelings of many of today's younger generation that he appears even more a visionary artist; and it will be fascinating to see the reaction of this generation, not brought up artistically on Graves' drawings as mine was.

Before closing, I would like to say a few words concerning John Cage's brilliant word-portrait of Morris Graves which follows. A lifelong friend of Graves, John Cage is, of course, a writer and composer of renown, and his work, like Graves', is mysterious and evocative. I know you will find this word-portrait intriguing and provocative, and I hope that you will agree that it is one of the finest pieces of creative writing to appear in a long time.

Graves' debt to Oriental art has often been noted. The Metropolitan Museum recently acquired a group of great Chinese paintings of the ninth to the eleventh centuries, and when I went to see them, I saw much in them that reminded me of Graves' drawings—the delicacy, the calligraphic quality, the sure and poetic line, the spiritual veneration of nature and our world.

The clear, gentle voices are again being heard in our land.

David Daniels
President,
The Drawing Society

SERIES
RE MORRIS GRAVES

The material of the following text derives from personal experience and recollections, conversation with the artist, one of his published remarks, and conversation with some of his friends, Dan Johnson and Marian Willard, Nancy Wilson Ross, Dorothy Norman, Xenia Cage, Merce Cunningham, and Alvin Friedman-Kein. Here and there I have introduced brief, unidentified quotations from *The Gospel of Sri Ramakrishna*, *Transformation Symbolism in the Mass* (C. G. Jung), the *I Ching* (Richard Wilhelm-Cary F. Baynes translation), Epiphanius, and Athenagoras as quoted by Hans Leisegang in *The Mystery of the Serpent*.

When I tried to imagine what it would be like to be Graves in the act of painting, it seemed to me it would be natural to vocalize and at times to dance. I then asked him whether that happened. He said it did. For the non-syntactical dance-chants, I used the syllables of names and words from *I Ching*-determined pages of *The Gospel of Sri Ramakrishna*. The arrangement of these syllables follows metrical patterns of the fourth movement of my *Quartet* for percussion (1935). It was following the third movement that Morris Graves said, "Jesus in the Everywhere." And it was the day after that event that we first met one another. After seeing Graves' series, "The Purification of Cardinal Pacelli," Xenia Cage and I arranged an exhibition of it at the Cornish School in Seattle (1937).

John Cage
Cuernavaca, New York, Plattsburgh 1973

SERIES
RE MORRIS GRAVES

TA TA TA giTATAgiTATAgiTAgi
The brushes. Before I went to India, he
told me: Imagine that you're dreaming.
Land around the lake rests upon it obscuring
its shape, shape that needs to remain
unrevealed. Path returns upon itself. Leaving by
the front door, we go around the lake and come in through
the back. Leaving from the kitchen, after walking past the reeds
at the far end, we return as guests
invited to dinner. In a shop he noticed the sato
yellow plates (a yellow between custard and yolk of
boiled egg). And he bought the plates not
for himself but for an eggplant he did not yet
have so that, placed on one of the plates, the eggplant might be an
eggplant.

Fire over China. But when fire died
down, behold, only the Buddhist shrines had been destroyed.
All else O.K. Then southeast Asia and Tibet. Nothing
about India. Egypt a little.
Unexpectedly, Graves was prostrated, forehead on
floor, in the room in which
Ramakrishna had talked to the devotees.
Presence. maYAYAmaYAYAmaYAmaYAYAmaYAmamaYAYAmaYAmaYAYAmaYAYAYA
maYAmaYAYAmaYAma In the liturgy of Hippolytus the water chalice is
associated with the baptismal font, where the inner
man is renewed as well as the body.

Rolls-Royce. Not just old: it was
vintage. It was elegant. It was the way for
those making revelations to be properly
transported. It was
necessary to leave the Rock. Navy air
training station had been established on Whidbey
Island. Flight pattern was out over Puget Sound and
then back over the Rock. Six, eight, or ten in
formation. The windows of the house would
quiver and rattle. garVIDyasaVIDyasaVIDyaVIDVIDyaVIDyagar
VIDVIDyaVIDyaVIDyasaVIDVIDyagarVIDyaVIDVID
ya No morning passes without his opening the
book. Day begins. There are
few markings. The paper pages have begun to feel like cloth. The
state of a servant's house will tell you clearly
whether his master has decided to visit. Purification. The
chalice is a fruit one half of which has
been removed. Old brushes
aren't thrown away. They become recognized in
detail. "O there you are." Escalator. Removed his shoes
and sent them up. He followed stockingfoot.
Choose any one that you want. Greedy friend took twelve.

Instruments for New Navigation. Constructions using
precious materials, marble, mica, bronze, Venetian
glass. To assemble them, he employed
Irish craftsmen. He was not satisfied
with their craftsmanship. Few have been shown.
JAI JAI maJAIJAImaJAIJAImaJAIJAImaJAIJAImaJAI
mavaSISIvaSIvaSISIvaSISISIvaSI
vaSISIvaSIvaSISIvaSISIvaSIvaSIJAImaJAImamaJAIma
JAIJAImaJAImaJAIJAI A discovery on a lost lake
shore which held, juxtaposed superbly, a need and its
fulfillment which had the intensity of a revelation. While it
occurred something was known anew
about where and how the best in life
transpires. Anacortes. We stood back from
the precipice. Beyond
it he danced on a ledge. Frightened he'd fall into the
valley below, we begged him, we shouted,
"Morris! Please! Come back! Come back!"
He didn't stop. Wild dance continued. The receptive brings
about sublime success,
furthering through the perseverance of
a mare. If the superior man undertakes
something and tries to lead, he goes astray; if he follows, he
finds guidance. Quiet perseverance brings good
fortune. Dive deep, O mind, dive deep in the Ocean. The
painting paints itself.
Child is born. Our activities are
peripheral (we make love; a pregnant mother follows a
certain regimen: asked to construct a
spine or brain or heart, she'd say, "I can't"). Third, the floors
are swept clean. Unless forced into the den,
he'll stay with the lions outside.

He'd been going through
my mind; then there he was as though
fulfilling an engagement. That seemed
strange. Philip told me it was even stranger: he'd not been
expected; he'd traveled more than two
hundred miles. Ireland was not noisy at
all. There were, of course, a few intercontinental flights,
but nothing serious. The problem was the Irish, the people
themselves.

SERIES RE MORRIS GRAVES

1939. Malcomb lived downstairs. Morris,
Xenia and I lived upstairs. Morris had the front room. Xenia and I
had three rooms: kitchen and living room halfway down the
hall; our bedroom was at the end of the
hall just opposite the bathroom. "What is your
favorite quote?" LI LA Temple of Kali: people frenzied.
Six feet four, mind a whirlwind, Graves raised
his arm, smashed his
offering, a tangerine, on the image.

Laing was telling about the people who had been
born again. As they were being
born they made strange sounds and moved in
strange ways. After rebirth they embraced one another and
were given new names. After World War II there was a
move on the part of many to suburbs. Woodway Park had a lot of
unsold land. It was subdivided. Suddenly all
around the Edmonds house there were the
noises of machines. He hadn't
told us, but we knew quite
well that when his door was shut we were not to disturb him. Everyone
expected something strange to happen. However, all that
Graves did was eat the sandwich and
pay his bill, get back in the car,
roll up the carpet and drive away. daSASAtchiDAnandaNANdaSASAtchida
NANdaSASAtchiDAnanDADAnanDASASAtchiSAtchiSASA The brush
is not an extension of his
hand or arm. (His hand is not that of a
painter: his fingers are not
exceptionally long.) The brush is itself a brush. It
is another member of the same family. Greenhouse off the
kitchen began falling apart. Irish
workmen (wanting two jobs instead of one)
had carefully put insufficient cement in the mortar. No sooner were
they up than walls began crumbling.

Show me about America! The country appeared.
Striped vertical aurora (red-white-blue and red-white-blue) along the
eastern seaboard. The jewel. I have never
seen him with brush and paper (twice he's made pen
drawings when I was present: once at a
Christmas Eve party when presents were being
exchanged; once in a guest book). The
jungle around the house is cleared up. He had removed all the
seats and put in a table and chairs so that the
old Ford was like a small furnished room.
There were books, a vase with fresh flowers, and so
forth. Wound. Spastic, like madman in the
street. Friend walked up: Stop it this minute!
Just stop! Spastic burst into tears, then roared with
laughter. "Thank you: no one speaks to me that
way." Identification. TRAI yaTRAILOKya Hers
is a female form. She is the Mother.

Spotted over the whole
country in five different places: great medallions of the
Founding Fathers. Washington appeared twice: in profile
wearing tricorn hat. Others had wigs.
Each time I touch you it is
you this same way. Dinner arranged so
two collectors who owned works could meet him. Wishing to leave the
party early, he used the excuse that they'd called him by
his first name.

They have a snake which they keep in a certain chest and which at the
hour of their mysteries they bring forth from its
cave. They heap loaves upon the table and summon the
serpent. Some of us are sentient, some are
non-sentient. All of us are beings. Once he drove
up to a luncheonette, parked, opened the door
on the curb side, carefully unrolled a red carpet across
the sidewalk. Then he walked on the carpet, went in,
and ordered a lettuce
sandwich. Meanwhile, a crowd
gathered. What next? How could you do this to
me? There must be certain stores where he buys
it. Or is that why he travels around the
world? The paper. He keeps it; and, once
prepared to set a sheet of it alive, examines each,
finding each remarkable. A party was arranged. The guests, mostly
museum officials, were chosen by him. They
arrived but he didn't. He sent a friend to say he wasn't coming.
dhiSAMAdhiSAMAdhiMAdhiSAMAdhiMAdhi
dhiSAMAdhiMAdhiSAMAdhiMADMAdhiMAdhi
"Floating world." *Sung.* Rain, curtain
of windswept lake's surface beyond: second view (there are others,
he tells me, one with mists rising). Yesterday,
stillness, reflections, expanding circles. A
western garden: water,
not sand; vegetation,
not stones. Thunder.

SERIES RE MORRIS GRAVES

Served him roast lark.

It crawls upon the table and rolls in the loaves. They not only
break the bread in which the snake has
rolled and administer it to those present, but each
one kisses the snake on the mouth. They gave me the
ivory necklace of skulls. After several years I sent it
back. It belongs, I said, in India. Now that India's here, I
want it back again. The lake is a cup
full to the brim. CHAI yaCHAI
TANyaCHAITANyaCHAITANyaTANyaCHAITANyaTAN
yayaCHAITANyaCHAIyaCHAITANyaCHAICHAITAN
yaCHAIyaCHAITANyaCHAIyaCHAITANyaCHAICHAI
Finally, the master himself
sends various things to the house, such
as a carpet, a hubble-bubble for smoking, and the like.
Friedman-Kein saw thirty *Instruments for New
Navigation,* elements for forty more. Told Duncan
Phillips how marvelous they were. NASA
invited Graves to Goddard Space Flight Center and Cape
Kennedy to discuss aesthetics of orbital travel. Came
to the concert with friends, a large bag of peanuts, and
lorgnette with doll's eyes suspended in it. "If
he does anything upsetting, take him out."
After the slow movement, he said:
Jesus in the Everywhere. That was taken as the signal.

Family saga: the animal appears. And he? He
disappears: to reappear in it. So when you see these things
arriving, you conclude that the master will very soon
come.

It was not at night. It was during the day. A vision of
various civilizations. China.
Tibet. Egypt. America. India missing. Going to the outhouse
one went through thick weeds five feet high. Once
inside, the situation was reversed: outhouse was filled with weeds that
were hanging from the ceiling. The best thing to do
is to leave the audience and go up on the stage, and there, if the
spirit is not moving, to remain immobile.
There are times, however, when it is necessary to
leave the theatre. KRISH KRISH naKRISHKRISHna
KRISHKRISHnaKRISHnaKRISHKRISHna
KRISHnanaKRISHKRISHnaKRISHnaKRISHKRISHnaKRISH
KRISHKRISHnaKRISHnaKRISH House in the
Himalayas. As they carried him down the aisle, his
face upward as though he were on a stretcher, he found himself
passing beneath her large
bosom (it was she who had given the order). She said, "I am Mrs.
Beck." Morris replied: Good evening, Mrs. Beck. He can paint on
any paper. One on fine
paper had been folded to fit into an airmail envelope. He went to
Japan to study the art of mounting paper. When all is
said, what remains to be said? "O lonely. O help me
across the stream." Long long
distance call. Mrs. Beck
followed Morris and the men carrying
him outside to the patio. The fast drumming had begun
and was audible through the closed doors. Morris, released,
began dancing. "His dance," Mrs. Beck
later reported, "was very sinuous." Bird's wings on
her head. The sacrificial bowl in
her hand. Having found him, she stayed with him until
he died. Suzuki.

SERIES RE MORRIS GRAVES

Extraordinary show of Japanese treasures. State Governor was
coming to museum's opening. No artists had been invited.
Proverb: Round outside and square inside. RA
His painting is *its* personality.
Skibberean (the gentleman's house) seemed too large. So when he
ran across the cottage in County Waterford, he took it. It
was smaller and easier to maintain.
Dorothy had returned to America. Richard had left for
Norway. The Rock. Graves was painting. Sudden sharp
knock at the window. No one lived for miles around. Graves turned,
saw beyond the pane of glass a deformed,
twisted creature calling for his lost brothers. It was months before
he had brush in hand again. Sri Ramakrishna not only
lived as a man, a woman, a
monkey: he lived for six months as a plant, standing
on one leg in ecstasy. Dinner with the Duchess of Kent.

Only way to reach the beach is to go through
the area where the redwoods have
been cut down. Desolation. On the beach there's a herd of wild elk.

Museum opening. Anyone at all who had money to
speak of had been invited. No artists. A distant relative
having an entirely different background paid a
visit to the family when they were staying in
Ireland. Stayed awhile, then went away.
He registered as a conscientious objector.
Drafted anyway, he was put on a train going south. He escaped,
'phoned in. Was put in the army stockade. Laying the fires. Log
across front holds fire to the back. Brick wall
reflects the heat into the
room. Otherwise, heat of the fire
goes straight up the chimney.
Taking out the ashes. Taking out the ashes. Laying the fires.
Friends in front: footman and chauffeur.
And the artists in the back: Jan, Dale, Patricia,
and Morris. Rolls-Royce. Aren't you sorry that you're
not a human? Edith wagged her tail
(Aren't you sorry
you're not a dog?). Who are you? Why don't you speak? Why
do you do this to me? What do you want?
The house is a chalice that has a lid on it and it is not
round. The garden's not like the one
that surprised Edgar Anderson in Mexico: it's weeded, clearly
distinguished from lawn and terrace by low,
stone-grey masonry wall. KSHA KSHA KSHA raAKSHAraAKSHAra
KSHAraAKSHAraKSHAraKSHAAKSHAra
KSHAraAKSHAraKSHAAKSHAraKSHA
raAKSHAraKSHAraAKSHAraAKSHAraAKSHAra
KSHAraKSHAKSHAraKSHAraraKSHAraKSHA

SERIES RE MORRIS GRAVES

"Revered sir, who is giving you milk?" "Brother, He
who beat me is now giving me
milk." Anything can happen. The reason's
this: any one or number of the elements can
remain as is; any one or any number of the elements can
change into the opposite. I must close the
door, for if I leave it open nothing will happen. He had time:
we never walked quickly; climbing was slow.
When we reached the turn in the stairway, he
was motionless, flat on his back, spread-eagled
head downward on the
steps, face streaked with dark red paint.
The scientists were pleased with Graves' proposal:
an amethyst on the end of a gold-plated boom. Talisman. Mexico,
Yucatán, the Caribbean, Venezuela and ten days in Rio,
Mauretania, Morocco. Loudspeaker (army prison
yard): "Graves! On the gate!" Sergeant
gave razor and brush and ten
minutes to shave his beard.
Graves didn't shave. Cursed and warned
him: "If in ten more minutes you're not shaved,
we'll force-shave you and your face'll be
like hamburger!" VA VA tiPANPANchaVAVA
tiVAtiPANPANchaVAti I said that music's
excitement takes place in public, that when a
painting's finished the artist sees it at once,
that celebration's reason enough for so
many artists turning alcoholic. He said
it would not appeal to him to have a drink
while working.

He arranged a sprinkling system: to enter the house
guests passed through water, lightly falling water, like light
spring rain. Seeing that he didn't want
the sheep to get into his garden, they cut a post of the gate
at ground level so that the sheep could easily
push it up and pass under.
"Sheep think better than we."

A house: private environment; proportion and
space. One should not reason too
much. You get clear water if you drink from the
surface of a pool. Plate.
TA TA TAgiTATA Shower's in the bathroom, not in a cubicle.
The opposite wall's a mirror. Steam
from the hot water produces the slow disappearance of one's image.
Pleasure of having a body. "Waiting for the gift from me to me of
death." 3:00 A.M. Irish tenor singing
loudly in our living room. Without knocking, having left
his bed, Graves entered, carrying wooden
birdcage, bottom of which
was missing, plopped it over the tenor's head, said nothing, left the
room. No further singing that
night.

Escape. Army command: Sweep the floor! He swept it
perfectly. Decision: he's not insane. You
couldn't move in the room except sideways and you had
to stoop. It was furnished with large tables, each with full
complement of chairs. Throughout the
room, heavy rocks, bound with wire, had
been suspended from hooks in the ceiling. It's said it was an
egg to begin with that got
bigger and bigger and by friction was burst into two.
The top part came to be the
Heaven; the lower became Earth. Aerial
relationship. Schlossberg: we are finding ways to transfer
energy by means of light, like the sun does,
rather than by exploding mass.
Sudden sense of identification, spirit
of comedy. He said that sometime after
we'd left, he and Ted Ballard got to
talking. Ted said, "The
difference between you and them is that they are looking for
solutions; you don't think there're any
problems." Your second favorite? The
Canadian Rockies. But not for a
house.

maSYASYAmaSYASYAmaSYAma

SERIES RE MORRIS GRAVES

The heavy woven wire fence is high and strong. It
protects the garden from deer. You cannot
see it from the house. It is completely concealed in
the forest. Cattle in the drawing room when
first he saw the handsome eighteenth-century manor.
Bought it. Against their
inclinations plumbers installed
three bathrooms. After carpeting was down, water overflowed.
Plumbers had stuffed rags and rubble
into the drain pipes. Magician. La Conner house was
a theatre: twice a month a
complete change of program. NA draNARENdraNARENdraREN
draNARENdraRENdradraNARENdraNA Compost includes vegetable
refuse, autumn leaves, clippings, weedings from the garden. Soil and
compost-maker including bacteria are added. Wooden
enclosure is taken down each spring. Same
wood is used to build a new enclosure. When I paint, he
said, I paint standing up.

riHAHAriHAHAriHAriHAHAriHAriOM!HAHAriHAriHAHAriOM!HAHA
riHA Asked whether he did what I thought that he did, he said,
"Yes." He gave me an example. He
can imagine having a house
in Ceylon, the Tea Mountains. Old woman dressed
excessively: false eyelashes, high red hair, trinket
jewelry. (Others tittering.) Graves came near: You're
very beautiful. She smiled, smile of light, "I thank you." Bird is a
chalice. Chalice is a bird. Chalice and
bird are breathing together.

His birds are not birds.
They are invitations to events at which we are
already present. Write it down: don't forget to reply. There are many
islands in the lake. No one of them is larger than a chair
or coffee table. They're covered with vegetation.
They are tree tops that have turned into receptacles.
Slippery clay-based soil. Eel River gravel was
brought to compact the road. Earth
takes five years to reach
the angle of repose. Each departure requires an
expense of energy. "Graves! Into
the Prison Office!" They had brought in the PX
barber. Beard cut short with
scissors. Then lather. Gentle shave. Like a cat
licking up thick cream. And have you heard
how he hit me with the loaf of bread?

He told me that weekend he would take the carpets to a stream in the
mountains. Stream would wash them. There was plenty of
water, and there were large flat rocks on which he'd
lay them out in the heat of the
sun. buRAMBAbuRAMBAbu The body's
a plate, as it were, containing the water of the mind,
intelligence, and ego. Brahman is like the
sun. It is reflected in
the water.

Mel begged to be allowed to shoot some wild ducks on the
lake. Since Morris was going
south for a week, he finally gave permission. "But only once
and never again!" After that, only the reckless
birds remained, and they at the far end of the
lake. His eyes had an indrawn look, like
that of a bird hatching her eggs. It may help if we try
seeing double or triple. Let's think that we're
entranced. Dinner: Washington, D. C.
Psychiatrist leaned forward. Stream of Freudian
questions. Graves finally put fork down, stood
up. "Enough!" To Alvin: "If you won't leave with me, I'll
find my way alone." They left. After these warnings,
signs of death will multiply, until, in
obedience to immutable laws, stark winter
with its ice is here. From gentleman's house to manor.
He lived in the house in FitzWilliam Square before
moving to Rathfarnman. FitzWilliam Square is
preserved by the Irish Georgian
Society. Front door: complex collage; photograph of a lamb
whispering into Pope Pius's ear;
mixed media. Sunset: Xochicalco. Goats.
Donkey in the great space in front of the pyramid. Wind came up as we
left. Circle with plus sign.
Plumed serpents. Next day
he put the circle with plus sign with his name in the guest book.
To do this he moved to another part
of the space. DE DE vaCHAITANyaCHAITANya
DEvaCHAITANyaDEvayaCHAITANyaDEvaCHAITANyaCHAITANDEyaDEvaCHAITANyaCHAI
TANyaCHAI

Some works are warnings. He's not just prophet
of bliss: he's also a Jeremiah. How many *Snakes and Moons* were there?
He pointed out the ones that had something. He gave no
feeling that he planned to do anything about the ones
that were lacking. Last February, however, he
said, "I will give that a little more tension."
Harlem dormitory (Father Divine): private room
(skylight). yaSANKAraSANKAraCHARyaSANKAraCHARyaraSANKAraCHARyaSANKA
raCHARSANKAraCHARyaSANKAraCHARyaSANKAraSANKAraSANKAra
CHARyaCHARCHARyaCHARyayaCHARyaSANKAraCHAR
ya New Zealand's Milford Sound. Fine for a house
except for the people.

SERIES RE MORRIS GRAVES

It is not always true that one decides to leave
where one has been. Sometimes one cannot resist going on to a
place where he has not yet lived.
His guests were not permitted in. But he'd arranged
matters so that they were able to
peek, to see that the party had already taken place.
West toward the sea, down the hill,
is a grove of alder. A road was made to get there with pickup truck.
Trees are cut down, sawed into fireplace
lengths, split into chunks. July to mid-October wood is
seasoned in the sun, then brought bone
dry into the shed. Passage from *The Gospel:* "I am
the machine, and Thou, O Lord, art the Operator. I
am the house and Thou art
the Indweller. I am the chariot and Thou
art the Driver. I move as Thou movest me; I speak
as Thou makest me speak." Where to
go? Twentieth-century's everywhere. He sees
in the night: he listens.
He sees as blind men do. Aerial
relationship. Noticing each is free to move in his
own way ("the worship in his own way"). Breathing.
Luminousness. Iridescence. KES KES KES vaKESAvaKES I was
standing on Broadway when you could still go both
ways. He was sitting in the back of a taxi. The driver waited.
Graves wrote out a check and handed it to me. He knew
I had no money. I looked
at the check. I was amazed at his
generosity.

maRARAma Just as the brush cannot paint unless it is in his
hand, so hand needs brush to hold. I asked him whether he ever used his
fingers directly on the paper. "Now and then a thumb: just a
touch." They sold the gifts he gave them.

It was the bump in the road, the old car going over
it, that brought the puppies into the world. Jan in
sequins, 'twenties style. Earth's
condition is receptive devotion. The earth in its devotion
carries all things, good and evil, without exception. We need
the *Instruments for New Navigation*. They must all come
out of their wooden crates. There are
craftsmen here or if not here in some other country
who could put them together to his satisfaction. SA
SA vaSADHAnaSADHAnaSAvaSADHAnaSAvanaSADHAnaSAvaSADHAnaSASADHAna
SAvaSADHA naSAvaSADHAnaSADHAnaSADHAnaSAva Work that could have been
done quickly was allowed to drag on and on. All
kinds of excuses were given. They
say one thing and do another. (Disgust.)
They're dishonest. Gaelic impurity: "There are
certain sacred parts of the body that are never to be
touched with water." He began to see
a lake, lake in his Eye's mind. The
search began. The color on the paper
when it was wet! Now it's dry. And then
again in Hong Kong: struck down. Invisible power.
What *Who?* Who *What?*

People and machines. Reduce or augment
their number of dimensions. That way's the way
to make them secrets.

The extension of pleasure through the house out to
house surroundings and, in an orderly way, into the day
itself. There are no engagements. (Preparation for
irresistible work.) Served him
roast lark. lahALALlahALALlahALlahALALlahALlahlahAL
ALlahALlahALAL The canyon is never without some movement of
the air. Its stream goes into the ocean. Its walls are covered
with maidenhair fern. Circumstances of the paper.
Circumstances of the mind.

SERIES RE MORRIS GRAVES

Cuernavaca. Osmosis. The smoke moving in the air, for
instance. We both have beards, full
beards. I'm nearing the end. I felt dizzy earlier today.
What caused that dizziness? Dark element
opens when it moves and closes
when at rest. The time's dangerous. A man
ought to maintain reserve, be it in solitude or in
turmoil of the world. ram ram
ramBABAlaBABAlaBABAlaBABAlaBAlaramBA
BAlaBAla He has refused. Perhaps he'll change
his mind. Invitation: to travel south to
make a series of lithographs. He was given a
pittance for the collection: one one-hundredth of its appraised
value. While you're in Gangtok, levitation, for one
thing, seems to be a
practical matter. (Mila Repa traveled in the air in the form of
thistledown.) This changed sense of what's reasonable
diminishes as you leave Gangtok. OAO:
Orbiting Astronomical
Observatory. Solar energy
absorbed by the glass-covered wings. After
their unfolding, a revolving telescopic
camera would come out to record the heavens.

He had bribed the guard so he might stay overnight in the
pyramid. He arrived at the dark appointment.
Then, recollecting having stretched out in the
sarcophagus, he changed his mind. Back to
Cairo quickly. daDAMNDAMNda He alone was served roast lark. Rock was
rock. No water on it. Every week
into Anacortes to get water at a gas station. Carried it in
eight twenty-five-gallon wooden kegs placed
in the back of the Model A
pickup. On the rough road coming home, water was
always lost. They fall down before it and call this the
eucharist, consummated by the beast rolling in the
loaves. Through it they send forth a
hymn to the Father on high. On his way to
Japan when he was in the army, Johns visited
the Art Museum in Seattle and was deeply
moved by a Graves he saw there: large bird turned toward a smaller bird
perched on its shoulder. Chain saws,
bulldozers, roto-tillers, powered lawn mowers. Then terrace
radios. Noise was unbearable. Three more: a yellow lower garment
brings supreme good fortune
(aristocratic reserve); dragons fight in the meadow,
their blood is black and yellow (inflation of
earth principle); lasting perseverance furthers (no advance, no
retrogression).

Change the shape of
technology. Shape it to allude to shape of a chalice. The amethyst
would be as large as a fifty-cent piece. On
the very end of a gold-plated arm fourteen inches in
advance of the body of the vessel itself. Talisman. Guide
asking permission. Receptacle. The house is a receptacle.
Each day begins the same way. Cup. Morning shawl.
The chair outdoors he sits in, facing the forest. The book. The bowl
of cereal. Morris,
immaculate, in tails wearing sneakers. Jan
in sequins, 'twenties style. naBRAHBRAHmaJNAJNAna
BRAHmaJNAJNAnaBRAHmanaJNAJNA

She could have helped him but wouldn't. A
few years later the skin cancer which had been removed from
his face appeared in the same place on hers. In one junk shop he
found the base of the shaving mirror, in
another ten miles away the rest of it and the
magnifying glass. You could tilt
it. There were further
postponements. "We must keep in touch." He returned
to Seattle. Received the letter. His plan had been
eliminated. No reason was
given. Letter: mysterious energy. Cable from
Dorothy Norman: Insufficient oxygen. You were very high. And
do you sing and dance? Not with words
but with the sounds that language had before it began?
He gave an example. Sometimes a word's included.

Chalices. Each of us having spinal trouble. We slept and sat on
boards. And laughter (next year we'll be in
wheelchairs). I was surprised when he told me that
he was considering letting any and all of the hippies
he'd met have land on the shore of the lake. "No one will throw
you out." SI SI jiSISIjiSISIjiSIjiSISIjiSIji
jiSISIjiSIjiSISIjiSISISIjiSIjiSISIjiSIjiSISIji
Which is the most offensive aspect of technology?
Its smell? The look of it? Its effect on food and water? Its
sounds? Or is it that anything anyone does with his hands seems
useless in the face of technology's lavalike
continuation? When the door was finally opened
there were drawings and paintings everywhere: on all the
furniture, including the bed; on the walls and the
ceiling. We had to walk carefully so as not to step
on them. The table had not been cleared. There
were scraps of food on the plates. Stem removed. An eye-like shape
remained. Bird waiting to be born. Deep in the Ocean. If you descend
to the uttermost depths, there you will find the gem of Love.
Go seek, O mind, go seek Vrindavan in your heart, where with His loving
devotees Sri Krishna sports eternally. Was Graves with us when the
earthquake took place? All the people who had
never met, even though they lived next
door to one another, met then and there in the vacant lot.
Conversed with one another.

Now there is no escape. Tanzania, Uganda, Egypt, the islands of
Greece and Greece itself, Italy, France, New York. The King of Sikkim,
Graves told me, has rare clarity of mind. He is a
devout Buddhist scholar. His
meditations are those of a guru. His
conversation's not chitchat. It conveys the best of
his mind. The more closely attention is given, the
more difficult it becomes to
fix something by name, or by relation to other
things. It begins to move on into
another being. Floor covered with sand. Large tree
trunk that'd drifted up on the beach off center in the room, ice
cream chairs in circle facing it. Cawing of the crows,
patiently trained, made
conversation impossible. They stayed where he'd placed
them: on top of the driftwood. Communion. The blood. He wasn't a
student. Why wouldn't they let him in the
school? giTATAgiTATAgiTAgiTATAgiTAgigiTA I suggested sitting
down. He said that way he'd have to have other brushes.

Unwashed dishes temporarily put out of sight in
drawer lined with silver paper.

SERIES RE MORRIS GRAVES

He filled a baby carriage with rocks and,
with strings, made a trailer for it of
toothbrushes. He pushed it downtown to the Olympic
Hotel, through its halls to the
main dining room. After placing a rock at
each chair but one, he then sat down and
ordered dinner. Seattle. They enjoyed an
immediate friendship. They talked about the mystery of death, the
nature of the next
dimension. Before long a certain
lightheartedness entered into their conversation. He could not tell
whether he was awake or dreaming or whether what
was happening was happening. Titan missile had been getting bad
publicity (two launchings had gone sideways into the
ocean); Pentagon feared greater publicity would
affect NASA funding. NANG taNANGNANGtaNANGNANGta
NANGta Second, the soot and dirt are removed from the rooms. In
this totality the conscious mind is contained like a
smaller circle within a larger one.

Petroleum fire. USA: red-orange.
Canada: forest green. Ashes. Out of Gulf rose huge
negresses moving like gorillas.

Has he told you anything about the actual
process of painting or drawing? "Work periods are often very
long, going through the night into the next day or days." He continues
until the spirit leaves. Portico over
the terrace was supported on one side by the house, on the other by
handsomely rough-sawed hexagonal tree trunks
used as columns. There was a pool with lotus. The school's registrar
was coming to lunch. Just
when she was to arrive, there was a knock at
the door. Xenia opened it.
Morris, stark naked, was standing in the hall.
Zosimos: "And everything will be moistened and
become desiccated again, and
everything puts forth blossoms and everything withers again in the bowl
of the altar . . . For nature applied to nature
transforms nature . . . all things hang together."
ra

They used rafts, piling on them duckweed and water strawberry that
had grown too thickly, moving slowly from bay to bay.
As they continued their work, more and more the sky and
the forest were reflected in the surface of the water.
Repeating what he had told was taken as an insult. He
threw the cup of boiling tea. I was obliged
to leave the room. The Duke and the Duchess.
Photographer looks at you but snaps
himself. Fisherman's transformed by what he
catches. Three tables? Or is one
sufficient? Providing it's large? The colors to the
left, the brushes to the right, the paper
directly in front. And the water? Surely it's here and there,
right and left, ready no matter what. Minnow
has put the egg back together again.
Amazon-like demonesses and nearly naked. They were replaced by
thousands of stick figures:
ants moving through the ashes.
RA maRARAmaRARAmaRAmaRARA
maRAmamaRARAmaRAmaRARAmaRARARAmaRAmaRARAmaRAmaRARAmaRARAmaRARAmaRA
Surface of the water responds to the
currents of the air and to birds, their floating, their takeoffs,
their touchdowns. My work is done: now the telephone
comes off the hook. Time for a nap before supper.

The footman rolled out the red carpet up the
museum steps. liKAKAliYUYUgaKAliYUYUgaKAligaKA
KAliYUgaKAKAliKAYUKA We fly
to place where no airplane is.
Secluded house throbs with
utilities.

SERIES RE MORRIS GRAVES

The wise man gladly leaves fame to others. He does
not seek to have credited to himself
things that stand accomplished, but hopes
to release active forces. He was offstage left, invisible to the
audience. After hearing his
wail, people were mystified.
They asked: How was that sound
produced? (Not who had sung it, but what strange instrument was it
that had been used?) Both sides of the windows
are washed. Windex spray and paper
toweling instead of soapy water and cloth. Variation is
introduced: some outside,
then some inside. How many
windows are there? One hundred and two.
Are you sure? Yes, I am sure. In the next box the
Princess Chichibu was sitting (Hirohito's sister).

A student needed money for trip with girl friend to Mexico.
Morris gave it; then asked the young man for help on four
weekends around the house.
Student agreed to come at 9:00. Arrived instead
at 3:00. Left at 5:00. "Nobody here wants
to work." As we went upstairs, I paused to admire
the charcoal walls, their sheen and texture. He agreed they were
beautiful. He said there had been a fire.
Except in his bedroom, all the walls upstairs
were black. For that reason he had the
house rent-free. Hong Kong. Day after receiving vision he heard
of the assassination of Martin Luther King.
Did both events happen at the same
time? A narrow window next to the bathroom ceiling
goes the lengths of two walls. It looks to the forest beyond
the garden and lawn. On its ledge are many more or less translucent
containers, empty and having different
colors. Floodlights. Guest list.
They reached the museum before the Governor did. I
stayed in the flower market. He went to look for
a shopping bag. I ate the
jacima with lime juice and chili pepper. The bag he had had to buy was
plastic. There weren't any others. kaLANLANkaLANLAN
kaLANkaLANLANkaLANkakaLANLANkaLANkaLANLANkaLANLAN
LANkaLANkaLANLANkaLANkaLANLANkaLANLANkaLANLANkaLAN
kaLANLANka

RA RA naRARAvaRARAvaVAnaRARAvaVAnana The world is of
the nature of magic. The magician is real but his
magic is unreal. He left Ireland, finished the
eight-foot wall around the house at Woodway Park, sold the house
and returned to Ireland. Nouveau riche: Letting
this wood rat in, you've devalued our estate
by thousands. Wife, however, invited Graves to dinner.
Tycoon's talk turned
toward view: artists are loafers. Graves countered: Look! All
you have and use (all of it!) was touched first by an
artist. Qualities of life he regards most highly: that
it flow, continuity; that there be concentration, no
interruptions; privacy, all
the way to secrecy; the mysteries of consciousness (he finds the ego
tedious), life as karma and maya. Helped by
a friend who stood watch, he borrowed the fowl
from the zoo. When we opened
the door, the fowl flapped its way in.
Xenia was terrified. Algeria,
Tunisia, Kenya. I told him
what Fuller had told me. "No reason for
you to drink: you're already drunk." He
laughed in agreement.

Is it Brahman's breathing that produces
civilization's changes? Kaliyuga. Exhalation. Making
matters worse. When will
Brahman inhale?

This is His sport. You must have
observed that all
the trees in a garden are not of the same
kind. His brother Wallace, far away, dreamt Morris
needed help. Up at dawn, took boat, bus, hitchhiked. Arrived at
dusk. Ten minutes before,
great stone had slipped.
Morris's leg was pinned underneath it. Morris
couldn't move. It wasn't that way at all. The
house has never been cold and damp. He
exaggerates. He gets carried away. I
wouldn't even dream of picking up an axe and smashing a stove to
pieces. Nor would I throw myself on the
floor. Each stayed in a lonely place until he
learned an animal's song and dance.
La Conner singing re-enacted the
learning. It was a teaching.
When others learned the song, the singer began to dance.
On a shelf on one wall: pink satin slipper,
blade of wheat, and perhaps some other objects I don't
recall. On the opposite wall: a painting
duplicating the arrangement. I touched both
arrangements in order to know which one was not
three-dimensional. jaKAKAliKAKAliPUjaKAKAliPUjaliKA
KAliPUjaKAKAliKAPUKAliPUjaKAKAliPUjaKAKAliKA
KAliKAKAliPUjaKAKAliPUjaliKAli Taipei,
Hong Kong, Japan, Bali, Singapore,
Ceylon, India again (two months), again Nepal (two
weeks), ten days as guest
of the King and Queen of
Sikkim. After dinner one
evening the King granted
his request. He spoke about the *essential* yeti.

SERIES RE MORRIS GRAVES

Lost in the forest, don't move around; stay in one place. That way
you will be at the center, and
the center will act as a magnet, a magnet for
those who are searching. The proverb, he said, was an ancient
Chinese proverb. Alan Watts hadn't
ever heard of it. The chaise longue upholstered
with beige linen was in the bathroom.
Lying on it wrapped in terry cloth taken from the heated towel rack, you
could look out the window to the mountain and harbor.
The carpeting, wall to wall, was grey. Nature
creates all beings without erring: this is its straightness. It is
calm and still: this its
foursquareness. It tolerates
all creatures equally: this its greatness.
Man achieves the height of wisdom when all that he
does is as self-evident as what nature
does.

BRAH BRAH maBRAHBRAHmaBRAHBRAHmaBRAHmaBRAHBRAHmaBRAHmama
BRAHBRAHmaBRAHmaBRAHBRAHmaBRAHBRAHBRAHmaBRAHmaBRAHBRAH
maBRAHmaBRAHBRAHmaBRAHBRAH And the way in
leads to the way out. Ezekiel 47:1: ''. . . he
brought me again unto the door of the
house; and, behold, waters issued out
from under the threshold of the house eastward . . . and the waters came
down from under the right side of
the house . . . .'' Kneeling beside the stream, she lowered her head
to drink. Had she used her hand or hands as a cup, she wouldn't
have been frightened by the snake that
appeared in the water to meet her. Wheel.
Pottery. M.C.'s poem: hands birds
(page's space between). Suzuki:
Hands Dirt.

maBRAHBRAHmaBRAHBRAHmaSAKtiBRAHBRAHmaSAK Twice we have
visited Fern Canyon. Earth above, earth below (K'un
K'un): nature in contrast to spirit, earth in contrast to
heaven, space as against time. Devotion. No
combat: completion. The coexistence
of the spiritual world and the world of the senses. We
listened to the traffic of the birds. A
highway. When the Baroness Mitsuko Araki was asked whom she
wanted to meet, she said, "I only want to meet
artists." He was so miserably treated he disembarked
at Cherbourg, and spent five weeks in Paris. When he
finally arrived at the castle in Chichester,
nothing but obstacles were placed in his path. The
dinner was the last straw.

SERIES RE MORRIS GRAVES

As we were leaving the airport Morris
said: First thing's to take a row on the lake. I said, "What
for? Mushrooms don't grow on lakes." Years later, Ted's
voice came over the water: "Mushrooms!"
Paddling out we filled the canoe with *pleuroti.*

We were in the flower
market (Cuernavaca). We had gone up and
down the aisles where the fruits and vegetables
are. He was carrying several that he had
bought and planned to paint. His eye
was caught by a large clay pot with a plant in
it.

I JOURNEY

Comments on page 68

II BIRD IN THE SPIRIT

Comments on page 70

III OH, WHERE ARE THE BRIGHT BIRDS?

Comments on page 76

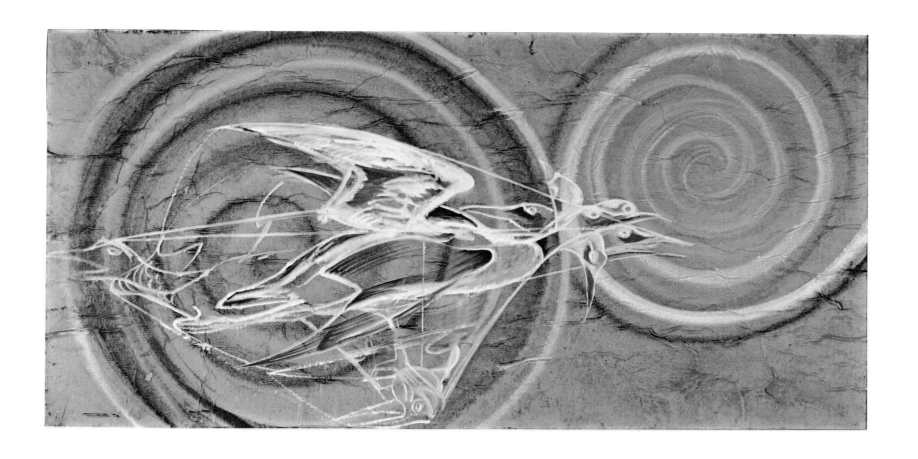

IV SPIRIT BIRD

Comments on page 104

V HIBERNATION

Comments on page 116

VI trout

Comments on page 140

VII BIRD EXPERIENCING LIGHT

Comments on page 142

VIII STAR OF THE MANDALA

Comments on page 146

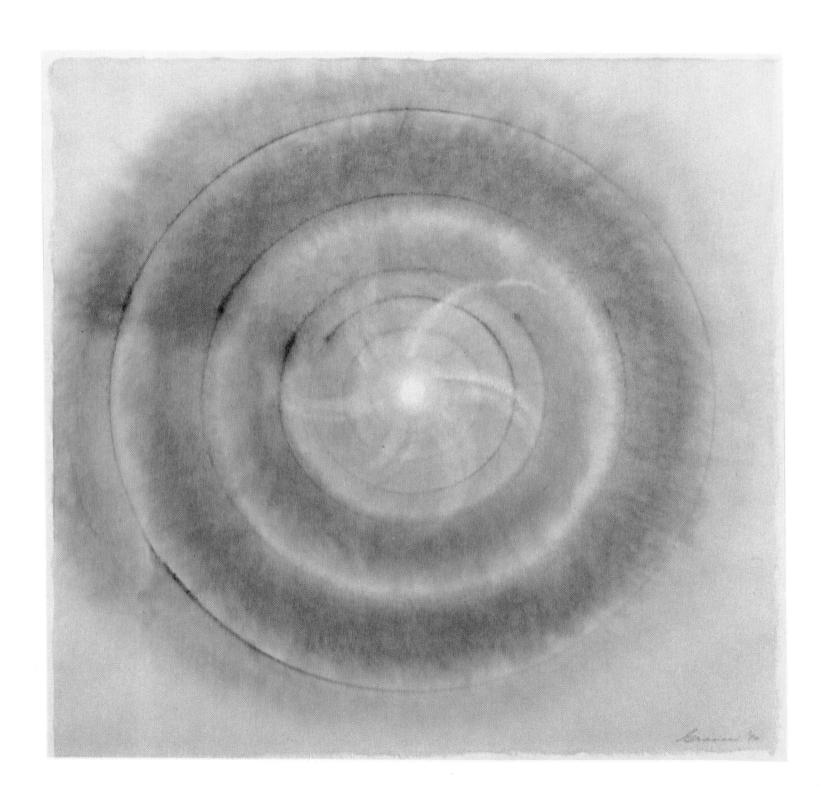

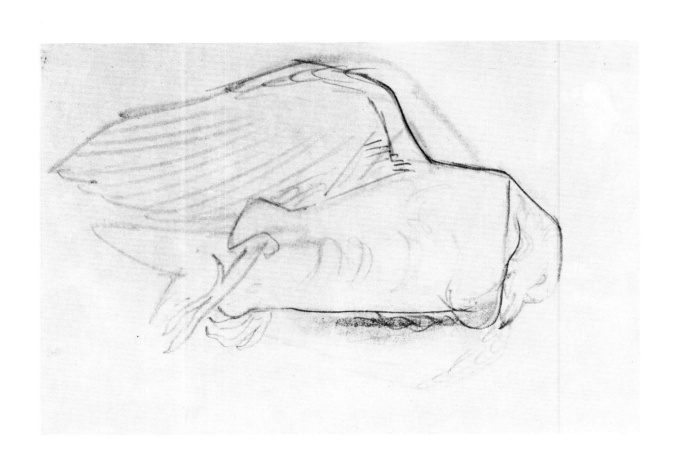

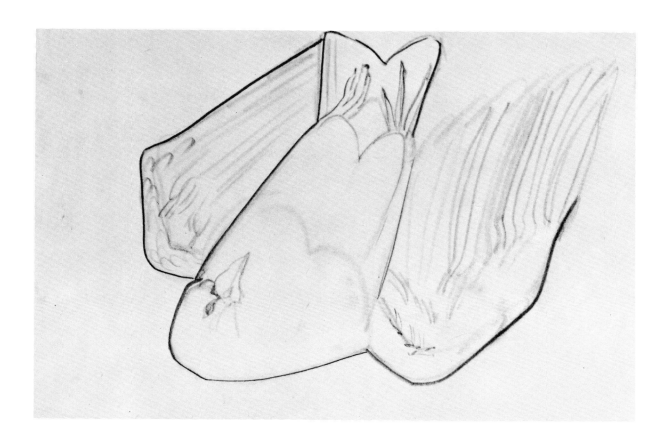

DYING PIGEON

1937
Pencil on paper, 10½ x 15 inches
Formerly collection Mr. & Mrs. Charles Laughton,
Hollywood

These pigeons would be a good beginning because
of the simplicity of the pencil line, and also
chronologically, because they were part of a series
done in New York in the thirties. I lived in Harlem at
Father Divine's and used to walk in Central Park, and
go to the Bronx Zoo. I felt a painter should resist going
to museums—this is truly a curious carry-over of
Protestant attitudes. But occasionally I did go to the
Museum of Modern Art, the Planetarium, the Museum
of Natural History, and the Metropolitan Museum.

ITALIAN NIGHTFALL

1938
Pencil and red ink on paper, 26 x 21 inches
The Museum of Modern Art, New York

Looking at the Nightfall Series the other day, I noticed in the "Italian Nightfall" the Fascist symbol, a bundle of arrows with a battle axe, the fasces, which is a Roman symbol of authority or military power. I'd forgotten that I had incorporated it into this Roman chair leg. It was a comment on what was being heard of the rise of Mussolini, the whole movement, and that was the symbol. Then the deterioration from that power support to this sort of Roman Senator's chair, being trussed up and reinforced with heavy bits of uncut stone—brutish, gross. They enriched the drawing for me. It related in some way to the shirts, costumes, hats, and those excesses on the body that still are symbols of tribal, stolid middle-class power.

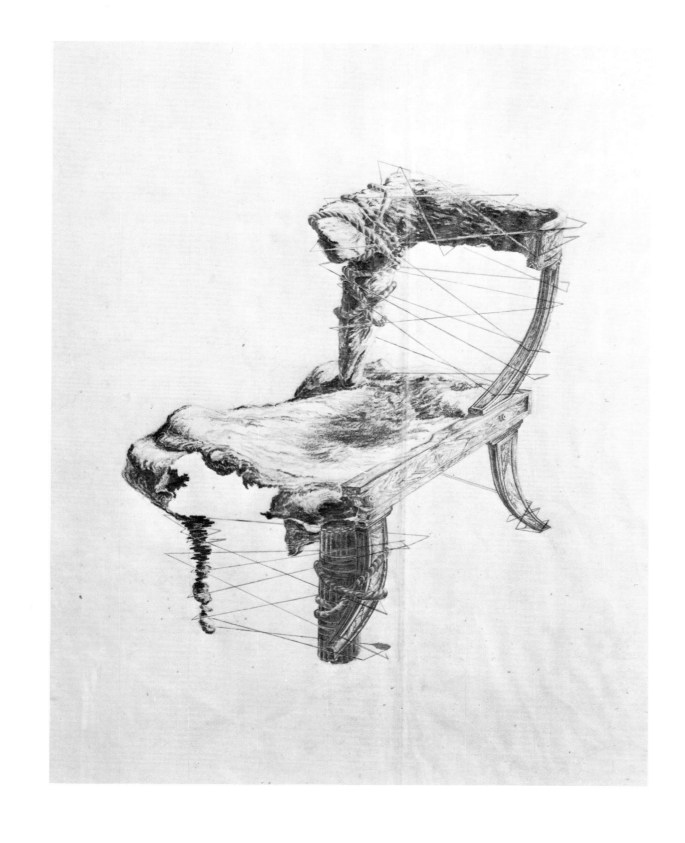

GERMAN NIGHTFALL

1938
Pencil and red ink on paper, 26 x 21 inches
The Museum of Modern Art, New York

In the "German Nightfall," the Teutonic cross, trussed up with a rustic, uncut tree trunk, had for me a feeling of Hun aggression. The little drawer alludes to the meticulous German attitude of mind for organization. This is Biedermeier, looking toward twentieth-century furniture—as a front, "Let us look universal, like members of the human family of Europe, instead of showing our true Teutonic roots!"

ENGLISH NIGHTFALL

1938
Pencil and red ink on paper, 26 x 21 inches
The Museum of Modern Art, New York

The "English Nightfall" was the most spastic because of my own relations with the Anglo-Saxon world. It's the most tortured. There was more anguish in the English decisions than in the others at the time, and I suppose in my mind it was Chamberlain who headed up that tormented decision. It's a Queen Anne chair; the eagle claw, which was often used in that period, is clutching a rustic stone rather than a polished, formalized orb. A tear in the eye.

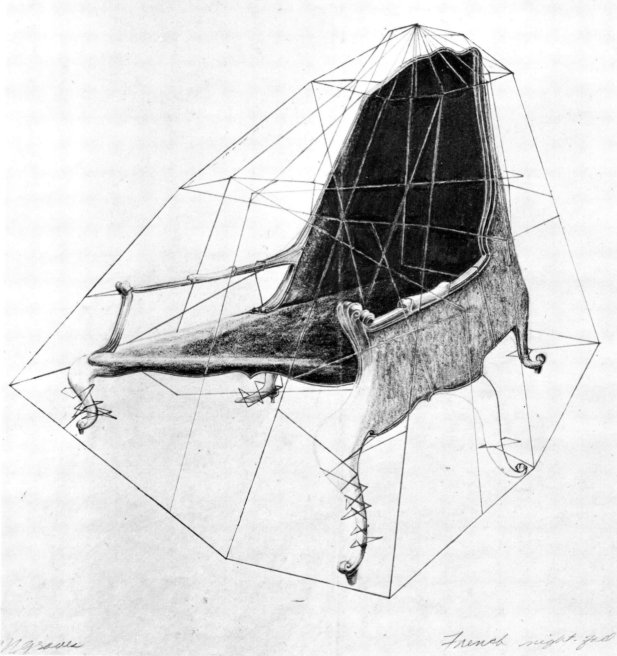

Ngraves   French night-fall piece

PAPAL NIGHTFALL

1938
Charcoal on paper, 25 x 20 inches
Willard Gallery, New York

On looking at the "Papal Nightfall," it impressed me that it was very accurate—I hesitate to say it—prophetic. These were comments on a state that seemed then to be present. The "Papal Nightfall" has materialized—the papal crown and crossed keys, and the way they were disintegrated and not trussed up.

Editor's Note: Besides these five, Morris Graves worked on a "Russian Nightfall," which was not completed.

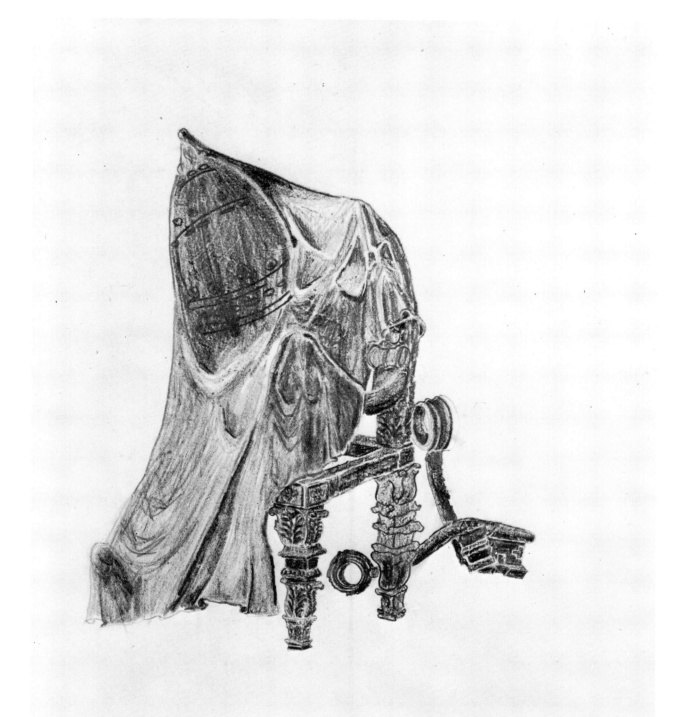

SCREAM LAUGHTER CUP

1939
Crayon on paper, 13⅛ x 9⅛ inches
Walker Art Center, Minneapolis
Gift of the American Association of University
Women

The date was 1939 and the drawing reflects the whole mood at the time. How could you gasp out a comment that really ended in a shriek, and have it imply multiple fangs? A deeper language—an archaic, primitive language.

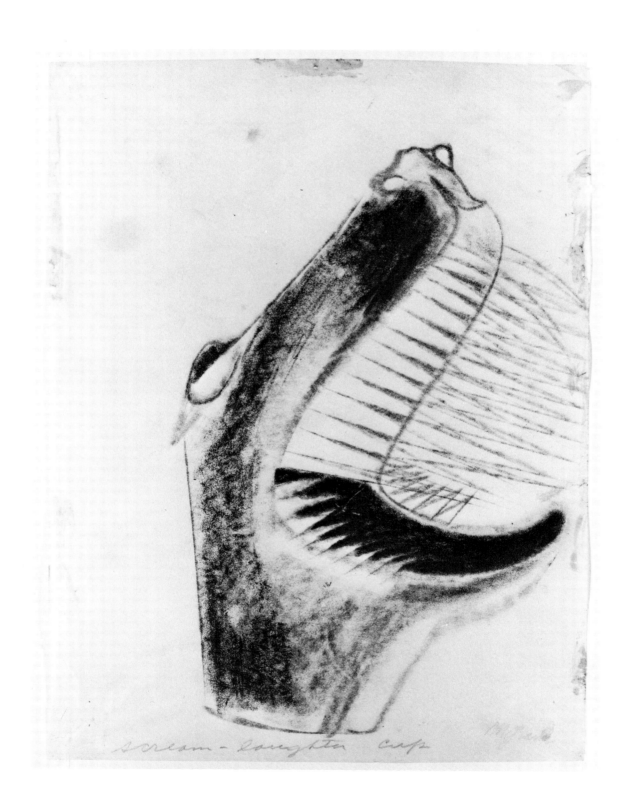

scream - laughter cup

SHORE BIRDS

1939
Gouache and watercolor on paper,
25⅞ x 30⅞ inches
Collection Mr. and Mrs. Alfred H. Barr, Jr.,
New York

I feel this is more concerned with the flow across the page, the movement of the birds, than it actually is with the character of the birds. I painted them several times and as any of us would, I responded to these little sandpipers.

TREE FROG

1940
Pencil on paper, 20 x 23¼ inches
The Phillips Collection
Washington, D.C.

This is a tree frog. They're those very fragile little frogs that don't live in water. I'd like a breathing space around it, and if anything carries through from the texture of the paper, to me it enhances the effect.

Editor's Note: Morris Graves agreed that cropping "concentrates" the drawing and then cropped it himself.

LETTER TO DOROTHY MILLER

1942
Tempera on paper, 26½ x 29 inches
Collection Dorothy Miller, New York

Hinterlands
Jan. 27–42

Dear Miss Miller:

P.S.
    I do not expect a reply on the above
remark on ~~fame (?)~~ acclaim (?)
Perhaps it's a crying fault to take oneself so
gravely.

Respectfully
Morris Graves

This letter-painting was titled "Stone Wings."

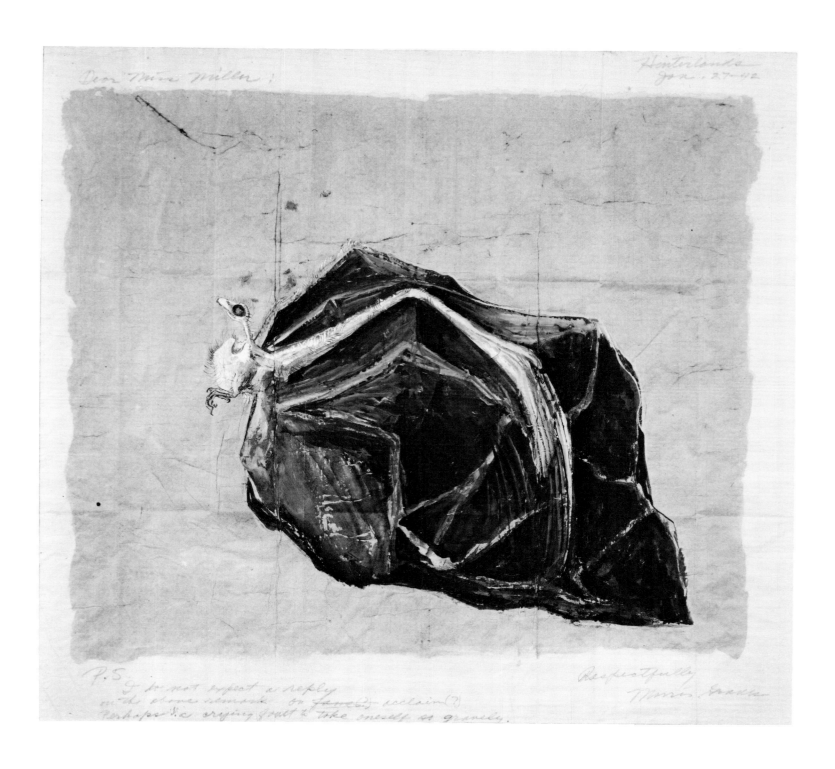

CROW

1942
Charcoal on paper, 27 x 18 inches
Collection Mr. and Mrs. Robert D. Graff,
Far Hills, New Jersey

By the time the painting based on this drawing was finished, it was called "Moon Mad Crow in the Surf."* The title was a statement of disorientation. Crows don't go into the surf, and he was not hypnotized by the moon; he was simply mad and just focused on the moon.

Like many of my things, the picture is a curious mixture of drawing and painting. I think of it as a painting, but as I look at it now it's quite obvious that my interests were more linear. There's not much volume in the crow's body.

From my point of view, it makes what I feel are the limitations of some of the drawings live a little better. The attitude is more in the spirit of what has been the painter's concern instead of a labored technical definition. These are drawings. They are in the spirit of drawings. They are definitely linear.

*Editor's Note: Collection of Mr. and Mrs. Milton Lowenthal, New York.

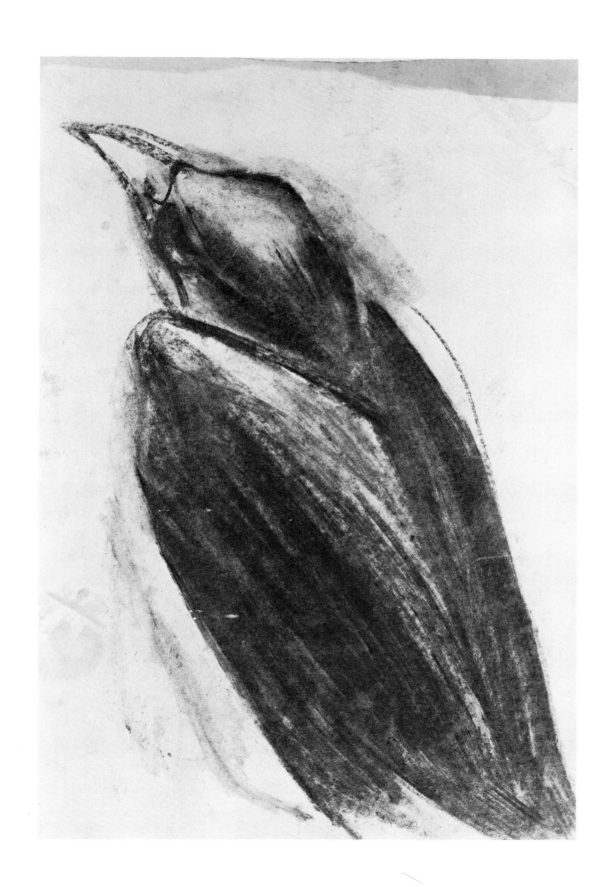

BEACH UNDER GLOOM

1943
Tempera on paper, 10½ x 22 inches
Fort Wayne Museum of Art, Fort Wayne,
Indiana

It's the perplexing thing of these fragile little shore birds being confronted with the turmoil of the sea and living with it. They are sandpipers, but the very diminutive ones are called sanderlings.

As I look at this—the way the waves are delineated—I think I was impressed with Tobey's "Modal Tide," painted in tempera, which had just received an award at the Seattle Art Museum.* He had so quieted the forms and yet emphasized the energy and the vitality. Also I was influenced by the way the Japanese formalized sea water, they patterned it so superbly. It could be both of these influences. I was certainly more aware of Japanese painting at this time than I had been five or six years before, and I would say it marks the beginning of the Japanese influence on me. I think it was the two-dimensional quality rather than the decorative that appealed to me particularly in Japanese painting. In the vitality of those two-dimensional things the emphasis is so great you don't feel into it, you simply see it.

*Editor's Note: Mark Tobey's "Modal Tide" won the Baker Memorial Award in the Northwest Annual Exhibition 1940 at the Seattle Art Museum, in which collection it remained.

RESTLESS INK

1943
Gouache on paper, 31¾ x 25 inches
Collection Museum of Art, University of Oregon,
Eugene, Oregon

We always project a form beyond ourselves, an ideal form, and "Restless Ink" is where we are at present, trying to grow to a point of articulation that would bring the perfected form, the ideal form, into being. If any of us in any of our experiences reach that point, then the ink becomes restless again, we project again our ideal form. Nietzsche writes that it is essential always to go beyond what we are.

OWL

1943
Charcoal on paper, 27 x 18 inches
Collection Geoffrey Gates, New York

Time and again I've tried to imply both the restlessness of birds and my personal feeling that one fixed position is inadequate to make the statement. When I first saw that painting by Balla, the Italian, of the Edwardian woman (skirt and dog on a leash),* I realized that you could compose without creating the illusion of movement, but somehow widen the mood of what you were trying to say, and this has something to do with this drawing. It isn't a notation for something; it was just trying to evolve—to suggest the spirit in this bird's body.

*Editor's Note: Giacomo Balla, ''Dynamism of a Dog on Leash.'' Collection A. Conger Goodyear, New York.

BIRD WITH POSSESSIONS

1943
Tempera on paper, 30½ x 26¾ inches
Collection Danna R. Dunning, New York

This is a drawing of 1943 for a study of the picture which belonged to Dr. Valentiner. It has to do with my highly personal and emotional, instead of mental, response to the state of the world. It's hulking up to protect a personal, minute possession. These are *my* seeds. I'm sure it carries through from the feeling of what was going on in 1943.

I like to remember why I associate Valentiner with it —because he wrote of the painting that I had handled the form with the volume of a sculptor. I was not aware of that, but handling it that way not only heightened the protective feeling—that is, turning your back on the threat, these are *my* possessions—but it also had something to do with armor. I was absolutely unaware of that until he mentioned it. But I was apparently unaffected, because I can't remember trying to bring volume to things afterwards.

BAT ROCK MAGNETIZED
BY THE MOON

1943
Tempera on paper, 24¼ x 30 inches
Collection Wright Ludington,
Santa Barbara

Our world in the Far West. I lived in a remote and extremely quiet part of the state of Washington. It was all stony hills, scrubby forest, and mountains that deflected every sound. You could hear the cattle, or a dog barking, from a great distance. The sound carried clearly, intensely. Living alone in that forest—kerosene lights, lamps after dark—you spent a lot of time outside, just listening and hearing what happened in the night—the forest creatures. That is the reason I painted this, because I couldn't identify certain sounds, and so any sound I could hear I paid *intense* attention to, and then quizzically and playfully tried to imagine what creature made the sound. Once, some years earlier, I painted my reaction to sound. I tried to paint a line of bird song. And there were some other sounds—surf—that I tried to paint.

SURF SOUNDS

1943
Tempera on paper, 26½ x 30½ inches
Collection Phyllis Lutyens, New York

JOURNEY

1943
Tempera on paper, 26 x 30 inches
Collection Benjamin Baldwin, New York

I think the picture states it. The substance we believe we're traveling over, and the substance we are, are identical, and it just heightens the personal feeling of the journey that we're making. We're walking through the stuff that we are. It's a rather rough and at the same time rhythmical flowing environment.

JOURNEY

1943
Gouache and watercolor on paper, 22½ x 30 inches
Whitney Museum of American Art, New York

BIRD IN THE SPIRIT

1943
Tempera on paper, 24 x 30 inches
The Metropolitan Museum of Art,
New York. A. H. Hearn Fund, 1950

One of the few paintings that gave me a real feeling of levitation when it was being painted and when it was finished. I haven't seen it for a long time, but my feeling is delight that the hand was moved so well. It doesn't hesitate. There is a presence of light that is sudden and vivid, like a comet in the night sky. You pay attention to it and then it's gone. The substance flows out from that point of light. That's the focus of the bird's ecstatic meditation, which envelops its whole form.

Bird in the Shirt
(from album sheet)   Hegedus '83

BLACK WAVES

1944
Tempera on paper, 27 x 54¼ inches
Albright-Knox Art Gallery,
Buffalo, Room of Contemporary Art Fund

This was done at the time that I had read Jakob Böhme and Meister Eckhart, and the picture stems directly from my painting in the Art Institute called "Sea and the Morning Redness."*

*Editor's Note: Collection of the Art Institute of Chicago. Gift of Mr. and Mrs. Howard Kornblith as a memorial to their daughter Suzanne.

EMERGENCE

1944
Tempera on paper, 16½ x 20½ inches
Collection D. R. Johnson, New York

The earth rotates and orbits around the sun. And this is a heavenly-body orbit bringing this combination of emergence from the egg and looking into experience, and departure from experience. That's why the hatching and emerging bird is used as a symbol, which is extended by the inclusion of the symbol of the bird skull, looking out and searching beyond the three-dimensional experience in the extension of the journey.

OH, WHERE ARE
THE BRIGHT BIRDS?

1944
Tempera on paper, 26 x 50 inches
Collection Howard Graff, New York

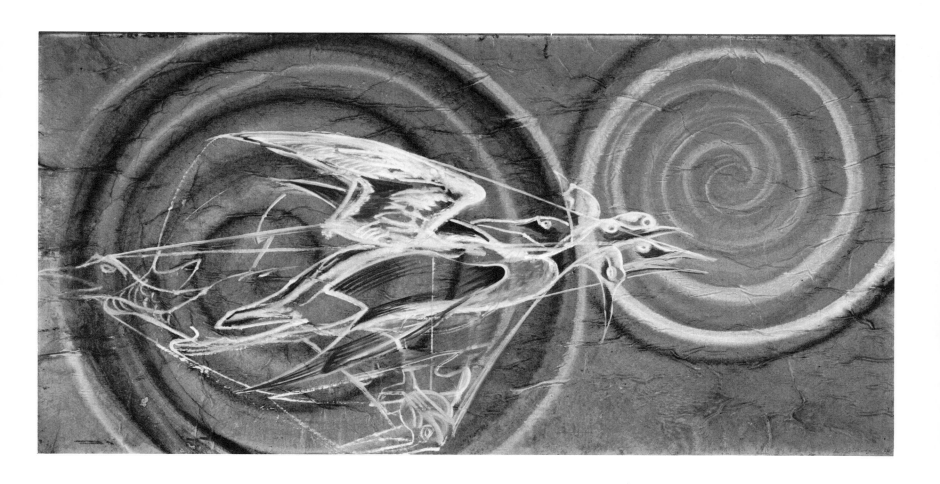

BIRD WEARIED BY THE LENGTH OF THE WINTER OF 1944

1945
Crayon on paper, 16¾ x 22½ inches
Collection Bill Baker, New York

This is a drawing for the painting of the same title, which is also a comment on the duration of the war. This was literally a drawing for the tempera that followed, done on that big-sized Chinese paper which was so rare. I had such a short supply of this paper that I had to develop the form before I painted it. The dishevelled plumage and the general feeling of the line of shattered fragility—almost no bones underneath it—was a comment on how neurotic the continuation of the war was making us—how unsettled and shattered and wearied by the length of the winter of 1944 we were. One of these drawings I rolled up and packaged and addressed to send to Prime Minister Winston Churchill as a communication. I also had things to go to Picasso on the "Purification Series," which I had packaged and addressed.

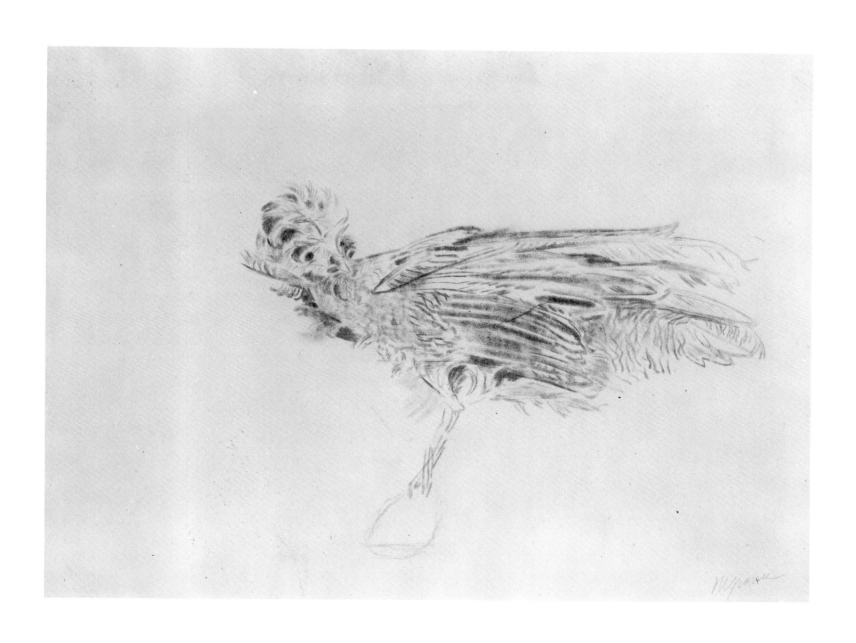

ZOO BIRD
SEEKING TO NEST

1947
Sepia on paper, 15½ x 25½ inches
Wadsworth Atheneum,
Hartford

The title intensifies the idea of it. The loneliness of a
zoo bird obsessively concerned with making its nest.

Just the weight of the ink I like too, as technique.

IBIS FEEDING
ON ITS OWN BREAST

1947
Tempera on paper, 24½ x 30¼ inches
Collection Mrs. S. R. Helburn, New York

To me it's something like "Bird in the Spirit" owned by the Metropolitan; it doesn't hesitate anyplace.

BIRD WITH MINNOW

1947
Tempera on paper, 24½ x 30⅜ inches
Collection Mr. and Mrs. Marshall Hatch,
Seattle

The "Bird with Minnow" and "Libation Cup" were the drawings that went into the bronze paintings. They are among the few that can be called preliminary drawings for some of the bronze paintings.

LIBATION CUP

1947
Charcoal on paper, 22¾ x 17¼ inches
Willard Gallery, New York

Unlike the other bronzes I saw at this time in the
Honolulu Academy, in which the history of the object
can be seen, these Kus couldn't be distorted, because
they had such style, such simplicity. They are not
fragments. They have kept their form. Of course, many
of the bronzes have, but these have a marvelous
power and presence—authority. As if they were
qualified to live, they have that life. And it was a
libation of wine and honey that was poured on the
earth from them.

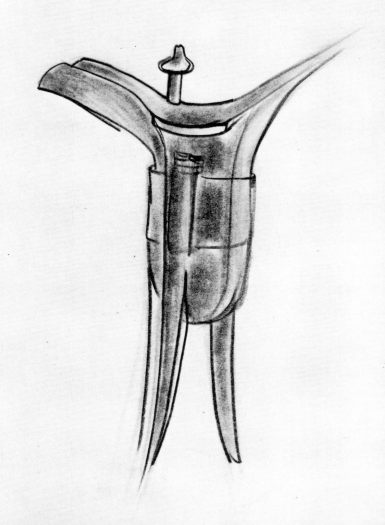

FLOWER

1948
Tempera on paper, 14¼ x 8¼ inches
Collection Mr. and Mrs. Philip Padelford,
Seattle

For Mrs Fredrick   Dec 48   J W Graves

BIRD CALLING
DOWN A HOLE

1950
Ink on paper, 13¾ x 9 inches
Collection Dorothy Norman, New York

Its title might be "Bird Yelling Down a Hole," but "calling" is lonelier, it's gentler, although there are many occasions when you're yelling down a hole too.

BIRD

1950
Wash on paper, 18½ x 25 inches
Delaware Art Museum,
Wilmington

YOUNG LOON
ON AN AUTUMN LAKE

1953
Sepia on paper, 24¾ x 43 inches
Collection Mr. and Mrs. Albert Gordon, New York

The sumi ink drawings are the result of a continuing discovery during a few hours of experience on a lost lake shore in summer 1952. That time and place held, juxtaposed superbly, a need and its fulfillment which during the experience had the intensity of a revelation. While it was occurring I knew something anew about where and how the best in my life transpires.

RESTING DUCK

1953
Wash on paper, 18 x 28 inches
Collection Memorial Sloan-Kettering
Cancer Center, New York

The Loon and Duck paintings are an attempt to convey
that eternal morning and eternal evening stillness
which falls over nature near a reedy forest lake. The
alert and evasive water birds, drawn with a few sparse
lines in watered ink, for me hint that untroubled
solemn stillness.

BIRD MASKING

1953
Charcoal, metal paint, and gouache on paper,
24¾ x 42¾ inches
Joseph H. Hirshhorn Museum and Sculpture
Garden, Smithsonian Institution,
Washington, D.C.

SPIRIT BIRD

1953
Tempera on paper, 20 x 30 inches
Collection Mrs. Baylor Hickman,
Louisville

The brief lines are an attempt to make it present and not present, seen and unseen—which is impossible.

EACH TIME
YOU CARRY ME
THIS WAY

1953
Tempera and ink on paper 25 x 43 inches
Collection Mr. and Mrs. James Schramm,
Burlington, Iowa

SPIRIT BIRD

1954
Tempera and gold on paper, 14¾ x 22¾ inches
Collection Mr. and Mrs. Donald B. Straus,
New York

This is painted on old Japanese Muromachi gold leaf
taken from the tattered gold screens of the Muromachi
Period and remounted under a very thin web of rice
paper.

NOH FLOWER

1954
Sumi ink and gold on paper, 7¼ x 11 inches
Collection William H. Lane Foundation,
Leominster, Massachusetts

It is painted on a Japanese prepared gold page. It reflects the mood of the Noh plays and the remnants of the Samurai Age, the fragment of a brocade garment, part of the tatters left after battle, so disintegrated that the spring flowers are coming through. Vestige of that period of opulence and military discipline, the Samurai Age, it is ghostly like the Noh plays.

ANIMAL

1954
Sumi ink on paper, 18 x 26 inches
The Museum of Art, Ogunquit, Maine

IRISH FAUNA

1954
Sumi ink on paper, 18 x 26½ inches
Collection Garland Ellis, Fort Worth

They are not doleful, and some of the other things are.
Let's put them in for the children. That includes
everybody then, for the child is in everybody.

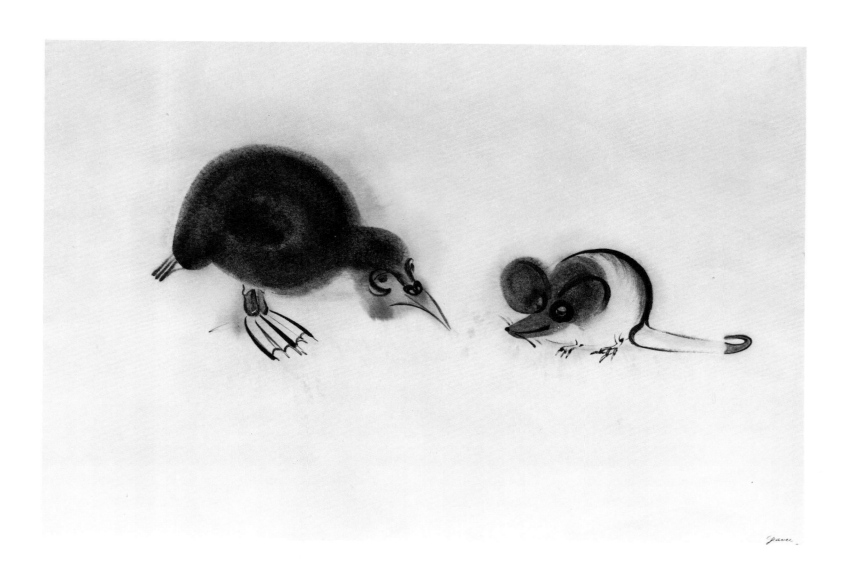

NIGHT HEDGEROW

1954
Watercolor on paper, 18¾ x 19¼ inches
Joseph H. Hirshhorn Museum and Sculpture
Garden, Smithsonian Institution,
Washington, D.C.

This has to do with spirit of the night in Ireland, and
it's not whimsical.

HIBERNATION

1954
Sumi ink on paper, 13¼ x 17½ inches
Collection The Bank of America,
Los Angeles

After a period in Ireland and then a return to my
studio in Seattle, I was again overwhelmed by the
machine age noise in America and was moved to
return to the quiet of Ireland. This is one of a series of
hibernating animals which were painted in Ireland and
bespeak a need to draw into oneself, into the quiet
of isolation.

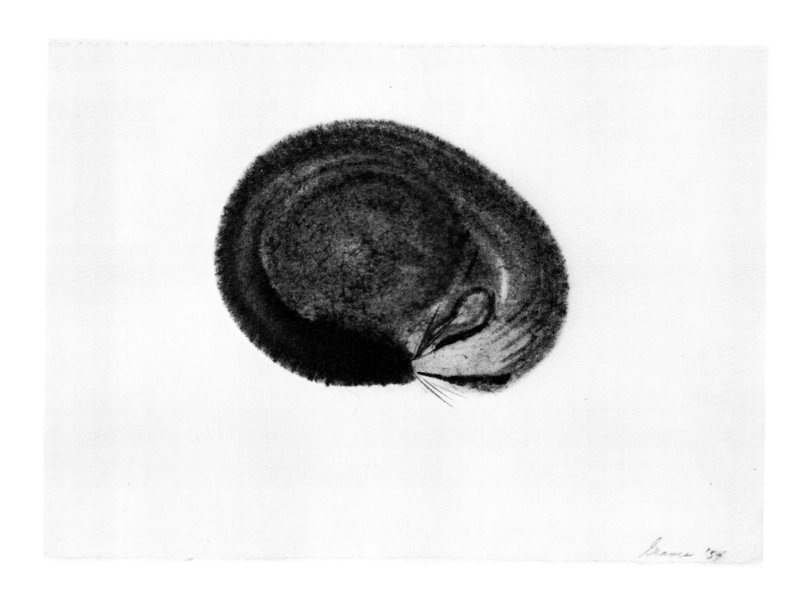

Graves '5?

HIBERNATION

1954
Watercolor on paper, 17⅝ x 27⅞ inches
Collection Sara Roby Foundation, New York

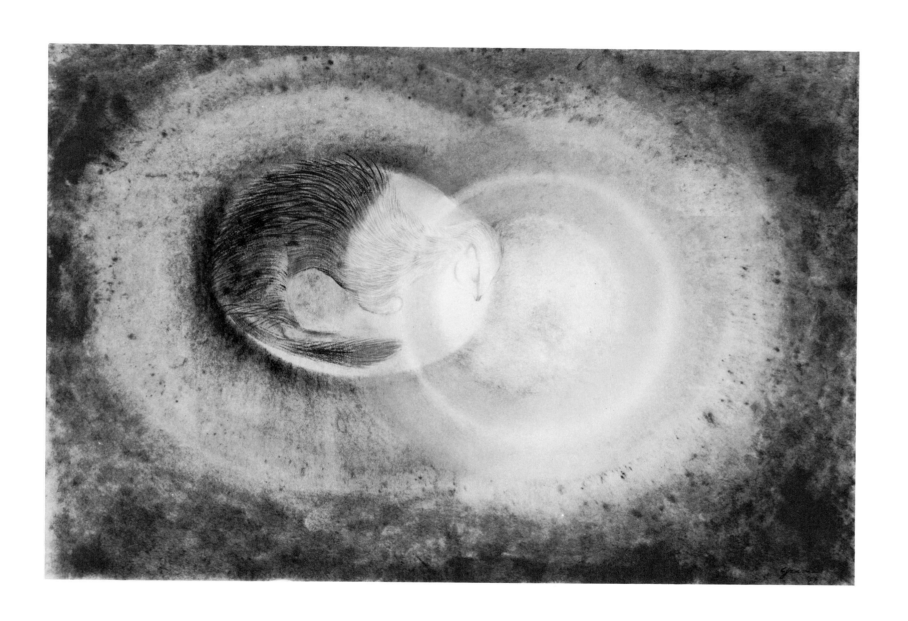

YOUNG SEA BIRD

1954
Sumi ink on paper, 12¼ x 16¼ inches
Collection Mrs. Edwin Graves,
Seattle

SEA BIRD IN RAIN

1954
Sumi ink on paper, 17½ x 25 inches
Collection Mrs. Robert M. Benjamin, New York

GOOSE AND GANDER

1955
Sumi ink on paper, 30 x 37 inches
The Joslyn Museum,
Omaha

It was a pencil drawing. I bought some geese in Ireland and they were in the walled-in yard off the kitchen of the house. I love the character of geese, and I made drawings—just notations—of how to compose the movement of them. This was done in ink. The one Alvin Friedman-Kein has* is distinctly a drawing, an exploring of what to do. It explores, it is hesitant.

*Editor's Note: See illustration, page 6.

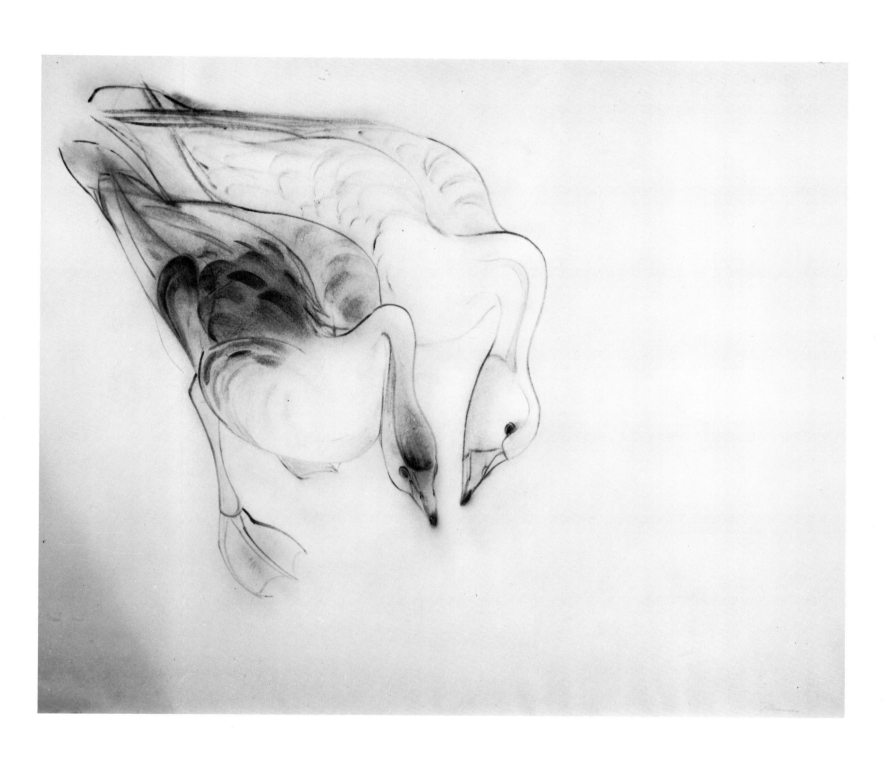

YOUNG GANDER

1955
Sumi ink on paper, 37½ x 24¾ inches
Collection Mrs. Stewart D. Owen,
Evanston

WOLF EAGLE

1957
Wash on paper, 33 x 21½ inches
The Dallas Museum of Art,
Gift of Mr. and Mrs. Lawrence Pollock

MACHINE AGE NOISE

1957
Ink on paper, 26 x 52¼ inches
Willard Gallery, New York

I painted all these things on the floor with a broom. I had a large enamel tray flooded with ink. I shortened the handle of a house broom to use as a brush. I would lay the broom down in this ink, and I would lift it up over my head. I would hit the paper with a smash which was a therapeutic release of some kind. It sounds awfully self-dramatizing, but it was a relief and a release to make a comment with this amount of equipment. There was no decision—just a smash on the page.

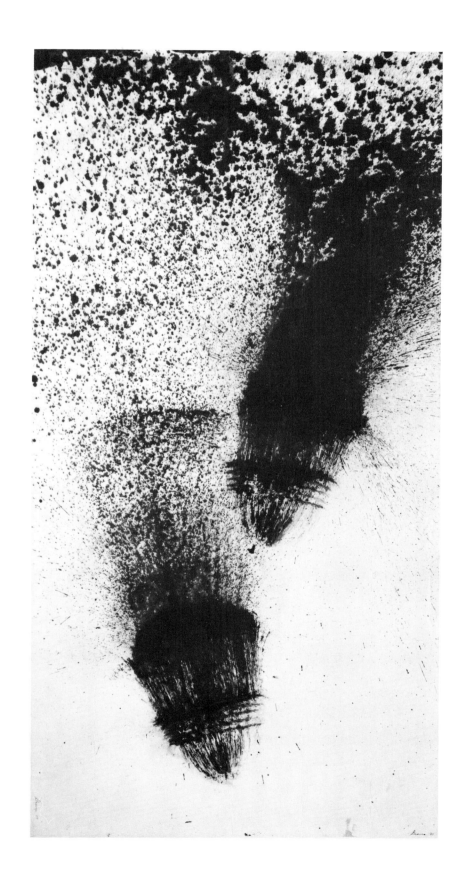

SPRING WITH
MACHINE AGE NOISE

1957
Tempera on paper, 26¼ x 53¼ inches
Collection Mrs. Norman La Salle, New York

The same comments would apply to this one, it is the same time. At some periods, primarily in Zen painting or in Chinese or Japanese calligraphy, there was a release of energy which is also related to some of our mid-twentieth-century paintings.

The idea in the paintings was that since the beginning of man's history he has lived in nature with only an infinitesimal amount of his own discordance marring the scene, but suddenly in our time man has been able to change these proportions grotesquely and tragically. There is a strip at the bottom of some of the paintings with a little indication of the movement of spring, but the rest of the painting is given over to noise—discordance—nature violated—aggressive machine noise.

MOUNTAIN FOREST
SEEDLINGS

1957
Sumi ink on paper, 25½ x 30¼ inches
Collection The Upjohn Company,
Kalamazoo

The combination of sumi ink and Chinese paper
suggests the environment of seedlings, the mood of
the moss, the bits and pieces which come up through
the forest floor.

INSECTS

1957
Ink on paper, 9½ x 13 inches
Collection Dr. and Mrs. Irving Burton,
Huntington Woods, Michigan

ANT WAR

1958
Sumi ink on paper, 10 x 21½ inches
Collection Max Abramovitz, New York

A colony of red ants and a colony of black ants, each guarding its accumulated treasure. Each colony's possessions are identical, but they are squabbling over them nevertheless. This is a comment on the economic element in war.

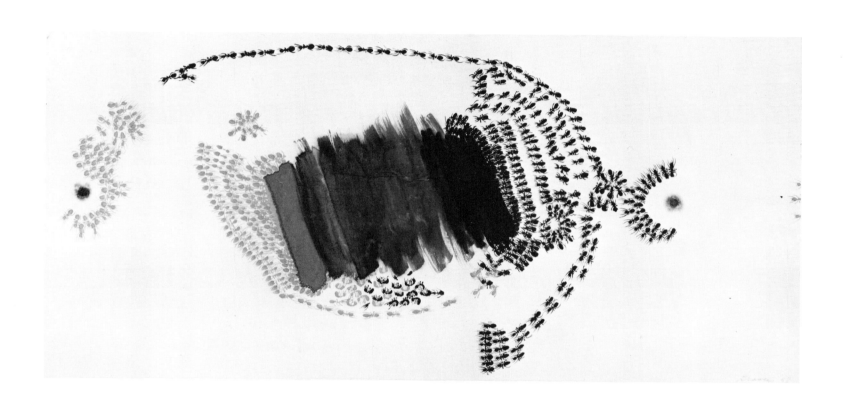

TOMOYE

1965
Tempera on paper, 9 x 12⅛ inches
Collection Nancy Wilson Ross Young, New York

Tomoye is used in both Buddhist and Shinto temples in Japan as a protective symbol—to protect the temples from that excess of energy which we call fire.

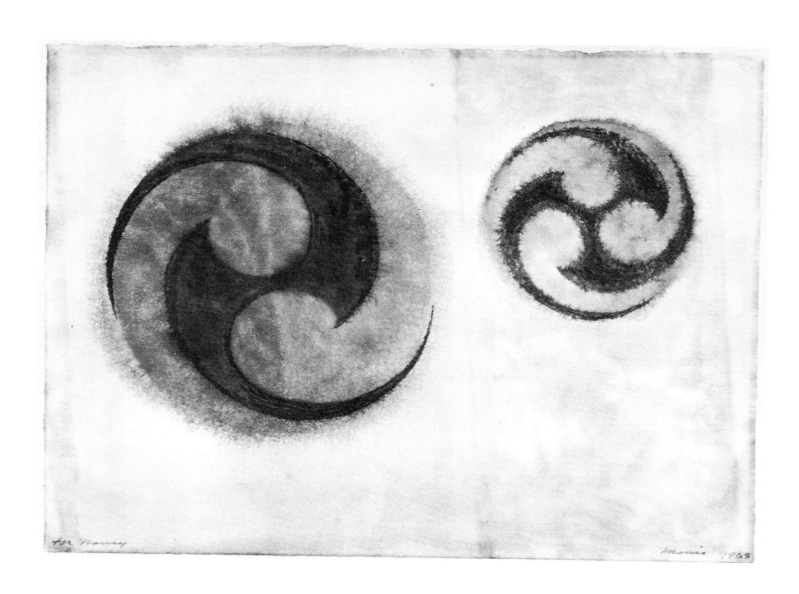

TROUT

1967
Tempera on paper, 6⅛ x 6¼ inches
Willard Gallery, New York

It is an image of the visual experience that is submerged, present and not present, seen and unseen, an area where it could not have been more distinct. Elusive, once again like the "Journey" in the stuff of what it is.

It is rare that I can look at what I have painted and say "no complaint"; so often one is looking at something that falls short. I like the movement of this trout size, I like the way it is suspended, the color of it. I don't think it is great, but there is nothing in it that I dislike. Very often there is something that you wish had not happened just that way—that you could have released it better.

BIRD EXPERIENCING
LIGHT

1969
Ink and tempera on paper, 13 x 10¼ inches
Seattle Art Museum

It is a kind of movement of experience that I have tried to paint quite a number of times. This confronts the oncoming experience which is painted, done in dark and light, the experience itself is dark and light, and this is the only thing I have ever painted in which the first view, the merging, the moving into the next experience, is expressed more intensely than anything else. It is unbelievable and somewhat odd. It is also somewhat whimsical, as though saying, "Wow, look what I have to go into," rather than what I want to go into.

ICELAND POPPIES—
A TRIUMPH OF
HYBRIDIZATION

1970
Tempera on paper, 22½ x 16½ inches
Willard Gallery, New York

Hybridization is man's imposition of a grotesque scientific distortion on a plant's genetic pattern.

STAR OF THE MANDALA

1970
Tempera on paper, 17½ x 17½ inches
Willard Gallery, New York

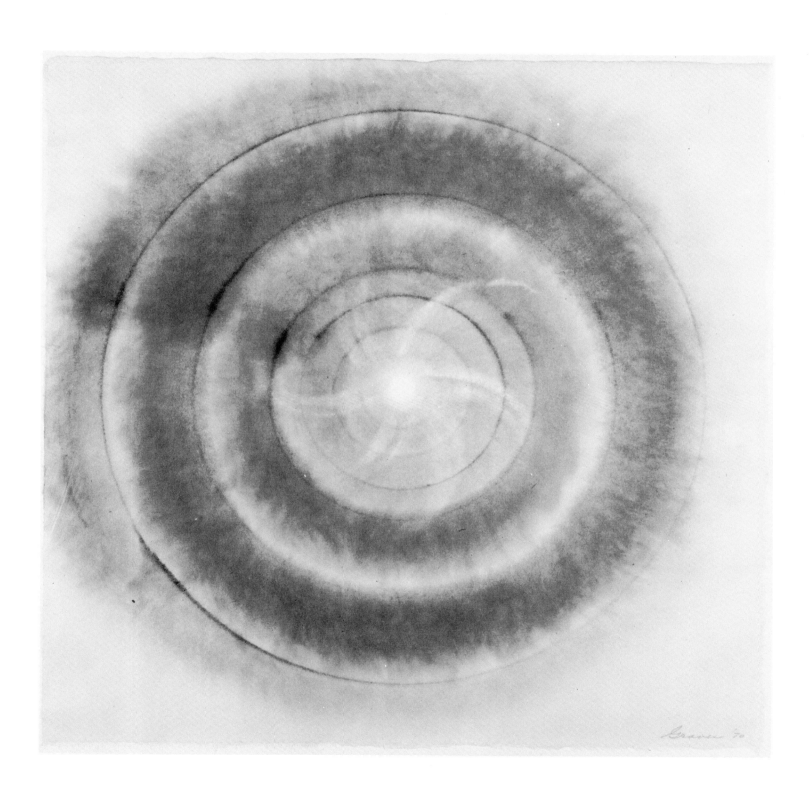

THE CIRCLE   VOID

1970
Ink on paper, 20½ x 20½ inches
The Philadelphia Museum of Art

Vitality of release is recorded through vitality of line.
Energy radiates from the center outward, as from a
pebble cast into a quiet pool of water. To use the ink
as tenderly as possible. A single stroke of the brush.
And to know when to lay the brush down.

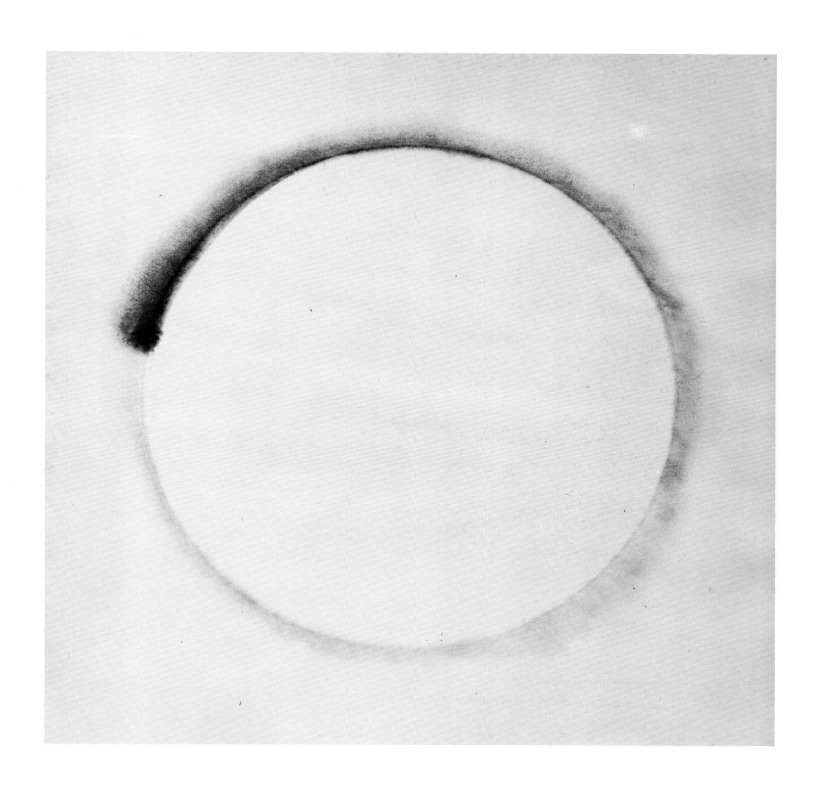

LIST OF ILLUSTRATIONS

MORRIS GRAVES

CHRONOLOGY

1910
Born August 28 in Fox Valley, Oregon, the sixth of eight children.

1910–29
Lived in the Puget Sound region, where he attended public school and two years of high school.

1928
Summer: made first trip to the Orient as seaman on the American Mail Line. Visited Tokyo and environs, Shanghai, Hong Kong, Philippines, and Hawaiian Islands.

1929–30
Lived with parents in Seattle for two more months of high school, then sailed as cadet on American Mail Line. Made two trips to the Orient.

1931
Returned to U.S. in the autumn and traveled around the country.

1932
Visited Beaumont, Texas, where an aunt persuaded him to finish his high school education, and where for the first time he received instruction in painting. His teachers considered him deeply reflective and mature. He illustrated the school annual, called *Pine Burr*, with birds, and was described in it as "A vagabond artist with commanding mien—a temperamental genius with precise accents—friendly—rushing here and there with flowers or canvas in hand—tousled hair—clear eyes—squeaky shoes—paint-covered trousers—and a large vocabulary to take one's breath away—truly individualistic." After high school spent three summer months in New Orleans with help of patrons Willard and Winifred Case. His visions of that city as a cultural center interested in art not substantiated, he returned to Seattle.

1933
Early oils in heavy paint: birds, animals, fir trees, horses, bulls, cows during the time he lived in Puyallup Valley, south of Seattle. "Moor Swan" won $100 prize in Northwest Annual at Seattle Art Museum.

1934
Seattle: with Guy Anderson converted a stable into a studio. Began building studio in Edmonds on family property. Spring-summer: six-month trip to Los Angeles with Guy Anderson. They lived and painted in a Model-T laundry truck; did odd jobs; tried to sell their pictures along the road. Graves remained in Los Angeles.

1935
February: received news of father's death. Left for Seattle. During the summer painted Sunflower Series.

1936
Worked for the Federal Art Project. That summer painted the Red Calf Series in Puyallup Valley.

1937
Painted Message Series for Federal Art Project. Visited New York to hear the lectures of Father Divine in Harlem. Made series of Dying Pigeon drawings. Beginning of friendship with John Cage.

1938–39
Summer: settled in town of La Conner, north of Seattle. Produced "Nightfall Pieces" as satire on Munich Conference. Autumn: traveled to Puerto Rico, with stopover in New York where he visited art galleries and Museum of Modern Art. In San Juan through March 1939. Painted Purification Series. Home by April. Worked in tempera and wax, also in gouache and watercolor on thin Chinese paper. Winter: lived in Seattle. Became friends with Mark Tobey. Four works shown in Federal Art Project Group Exhibition at Museum of Modern Art in New York.

1940
Spring: built cabin on Fidalgo, one of the San Juan Islands in Puget Sound nearest to La Conner. The site: a stony plateau with magnificent views, named The Rock. September: on staff of Seattle Art Museum full time until Christmas. Attachment to Museum continued until 1942.

1941
Painted Inner Eye Series at The Rock. His new work seen in Seattle by Dorothy Miller of The Museum of Modern Art who included him in the exhibition "18 Americans from 9 States" the following year.

1942
Registered under Selective Service Act as Conscientious Objector. Draft board refused C.O. classification because he was "not a member of a peace group or pacifist church." Was sent notice for induction; refused induction and was held in an Army guardhouse until released eleven months later as "unadaptable for military service."

1943
Discharged from Army in April. Returned to The Rock, where he expanded original shack into a camp. At first painted dark moody birds, wounded gulls, plovers by the sea, and night scenes; then painted Journey Series and Joyous Young Pine Series.

1944
Continued to paint Joyous Young Pine Series; painted Old Pine Top Series and Leaf Series.

1945
Painted Crane Series.

1946–47
Awarded a Guggenheim Fellowship for study in Japan; traveled as far as Honolulu; military permit for civilian to enter Japan withheld. Painted Chinese Bronze Series. On return to U.S., moved from The Rock; began building new home in Edmonds with help of Japanese painter Yone Arashiro. Norman Wait Harris Medal from Art Institute of Chicago for "Black Waves."

1948–49
Summer: trip to Europe on invitation of collector Edward James. England and France, winter in Chartres, brief trip to Italy before returning to Edmonds in the spring. Destroyed paintings from Chartres. Watson F. Blair Prize from Art Institute of Chicago for "In the Air." Painted Bouquet Series.

1950
Six-month trip to Mexico.

1952–53
Returned to painting large oils.

1954
Summer: completed house at Edmonds. Autumn: trip to Japan and later went to live in County Cork, Ireland. Painted Hibernating Animals.

1955
University of Illinois Purchase Prize.

1956
Returned to Seattle. Received grant from National Institute of Arts and Letters.

1957
Painted Spring With Machine Age Noise Series. Elected a member of the National Institute of Arts and Letters. Won first Windsor Award for study in Europe. Spent one month in Paris, visited Norway, and returned to Ireland.

1958
Painted Ant War Series and Insect Series. Traveled in Europe.

1959–60
Bought a house in Ireland.

1961–62
Embarked on a trip around the world.

1963
Traveled in India and Japan.

1964
Returned to U.S. and bought property near Loleta, in northern California, where he now lives.

1968
October: elected an Honorary Member of American Watercolor Society.

1971
Travel in Asia.

1972
Travel in Africa and South America.

1973
Travel in Far East, including Burma and Nepal.

EXHIBITIONS

Morris Graves exhibited frequently in the Whitney Annual, at the Willard Gallery, and at the Ogunquit Museum of Art, but because of space limitations below, these references are grouped under the earliest listing. For the Whitney Annual and Willard Gallery, see 1942; for Ogunquit, see 1956.

One-man exhibitions are marked with an asterisk and precede group shows for each year.

1936
*Seattle Art Museum

1939
Seattle Art Museum
The Museum of Modern Art, New York. Group show representing artists connected with the Federal Art Project

1942
*Willard Gallery, New York. The first exhibition of Graves's work at the gallery with which he is still affiliated. (Succeeding one-man shows were held at the Willard Gallery in 1944, 1945, 1948, 1954, 1955, 1959, 1968, 1971, 1972, and 1973)
The Museum of Modern Art, New York. "18 Americans from 9 States"
The Phillips Collection, Washington, D.C. "Three Americans: Weber, Knaths, Graves"
Whitney Museum of American Art, New York. "Annual Exhibition." (Graves' work was exhibited at the Whitney every year from this year through 1967)

1943
*Arts Club of Chicago
*University Gallery, Minneapolis
*Detroit Institute of Arts
*Phillips Collection, Washington, D.C.
The Museum of Modern Art, New York. "Romantic Painting in America"
University of Nebraska, Lincoln
Art Institute of Chicago
Kalamazoo Institute of Arts, "Fantasy"

1944
Chicago Art Institute. "Abstract and Surrealist Art"
Detroit Institute of Arts. "Advance Trends in Contemporary American Art"

1945
Pennsylvania Academy of the Fine Arts, Philadelphia
The Brooklyn Museum
American Federation of Arts (traveling exhibition)

1946
*Philadelphia Art Alliance
Tate Gallery, London. "American Painting of the 20th Century"
Detroit Institute of Arts. "American Birds and Their Painters and Sculptors"

1948
*California Palace of the Legion of Honor, San Francisco (retrospective)
*Santa Barbara Museum
*Los Angeles County Museum
Art Institute of Chicago. "Annual American Exhibition"
Iowa State University, Des Moines
University of Nebraska, Lincoln
Colorado Springs Fine Arts Center. "Artists West of the Mississippi"
Wadsworth Atheneum, Hartford. "Seven by Six: Contemporary American Water Colors"
Baltimore Museum of Art. "Ten Painters of the Pacific Northwest"
Buchholz Gallery, New York. "Drawings and Watercolors from the Collection of John S. Newberry Jr."

1949
Kootz Gallery, New York. "The Intransubjectives"
Art Institute of Chicago. "Annual Exhibition"

1950
*Margaret Brown Gallery, Boston

1951
São Paulo, Brazil. "Biennial Exhibition"

1952
*Beaumont Art Museum, Beaumont, Texas
Cincinnati Art Museum. "Modern Art Society: Purchase Exhibition"
Albright-Knox Art Gallery, Buffalo. "Expressionism in Modern Painting"

University of Illinois, Urbana, College of Fine and Applied Arts. "Collection of Contemporary American Painting and Sculpture"
Mayo Hill Galleries, Wellfleet, Massachusetts. "Morris Graves, Gyorgy Kepes, Mark Tobey"
Kunstsammlungen der Stadt Düsseldorf. "Zwölf Americanische Maler und Bildhauer der Gegenwart"

1953

Public Library, Winston-Salem, North Carolina. "Musical Themes" (organized by The Museum of Modern Art, New York)
Art Institute of Chicago. "Contemporary Drawings from Twelve Countries"
Wildenstein Gallery, New York. "Landmarks of Three Centuries"
Stockholm Museum. "Tolv Nutida Amerikanske Malere och Skulpturen"

1954

Phillips Collection, Washington, D.C. "Loan Exhibition"
Paris, Museé National d'Art Moderne. "Le Dessin Contemporain aux Etats-Unis"
Bordeaux, Salle Franklin. "L'Aquarelle Contemporain aux Etats-Unis"
Oslo Museum. "Tolv Amerikanske Malere ag Billedhuggere"
Art Institute of Chicago. "61st American Exhibition: Paintings and Sculpture"
Walker Art Center, Minneapolis. "Reality and Fantasy"

1955

*Otto Seligman Gallery, Seattle (courtesy Willard Gallery)
*Oslo Kunstforening
Carnegie Institute, Pittsburgh. "International Exhibition"
University of Illinois, Urbana. "Exhibition of Contemporary American Painting"
San Francisco Museum of Art, "Art in the Twentieth Century"
Syracuse Museum of Art, Syracuse, New York. "Contemporary Painting"

1956

*Art Galleries, University of California at Los Angeles. Retrospective exhibition (see Bibliography for list of participating institutions)
*Landau Gallery, Los Angeles
The Museum of Modern Art, New York. "Recent Drawings, U.S.A."
Spook Farm Gallery, Far Hills, New Jersey. "Current Trends in American Painting"

Ogunquit Museum of Art. "Fourth Annual Exhibition." (Works by Graves were also included in Ogunquit's Annuals for 1957, 1958, 1961, and 1967)
Contemporary Arts Museum, Houston, Texas. "Contemporary Calligraphers"

1957

*Bridgestone Gallery, Tokyo. Retrospective exhibition
The Brooklyn Museum. "Golden Years of American Drawings, 1905–1956"
University of Illinois, Urbana. "Twentieth Century Works of Art"
Randolph-Macon Woman's College, Lynchburg, Virginia. "46th Annual Exhibition of American Painting"
Seattle Art Museum. "Four Seattle Painters: Tobey, Graves, Callahan, Anderson." (This exhibition was sent abroad under the auspices of the United States Information Agency)
Château Historique de la Napoule, France, Henry Clews Memorial. "Cinq Maîtres de la Ligne"
Minneapolis Institute of Arts. "American Paintings 1945–57"

1958

*Fairweather-Hardin Gallery, Chicago
Brussels World's Fair
Montreal Museum of Fine Arts. "Contemporary American Painters"
Denver Art Museum. "Collectors' Choice for 1958"
Dallas Museum of Fine Arts. "Famous Paintings and Famous Painters"
DuPont Galleries, Wilmington. "Third Annual Exhibition of Contemporary Painting"

1959

Moscow Fair. "American National Exhibition"

1960

Denver Art Museum. "Collectors' Choice for 1960"
Isaac Delgado Museum of Art, New Orleans. "The World of Art in 1910"

1961

*New York Foundation, Rome
*Bezalel National Museum, Jerusalem
Randolph-Macon Woman's College, Lynchburg, Virginia. "Artists on Our Want List"
Museum of Modern Art, Rome. "Disegni Americani Moderni"

Dallas Museum of Fine Arts. "Directions in Twentieth Century American Painting"

1962

Munson-Williams-Proctor Institute, Utica, New York. "Edward Wales Root Bequest"

Whitney Museum of American Art, New York. "Masters of American Water Color" (traveling exhibition sponsored by the New York State Council on the Arts and circulated by the American Federation of Arts)

Mary Washington College of the University of Virginia, Fredericksburg. "7th Annual International Exhibition of Modern Art"

Institute of Contemporary Art, Boston. "American Art since 1950" (sponsored by Poses Institute of Fine Arts, Brandeis University, Waltham, Massachusetts)

"The Artist's Environment: West Coast," an exhibition shown at the Amon Carter Museum of Western Art, Fort Worth, Texas; the Art Galleries of the University of California at Los Angeles; and the Oakland Art Museum, Oakland, California

Seattle World's Fair. "The First Five Years" (organized by the Whitney Museum of American Art, New York)

1963

*Pavilion Gallery, Balboa, California. Retrospective exhibition

*St. Paul Art Center, St. Paul, Minnesota

Allan Stone Gallery, New York. Exhibition and sale of works of Art Donated by Artists to the Foundation for the Contemporary Performance Arts

Pennsylvania Academy of the Fine Arts, Philadelphia. "158th Annual Exhibition"

Columbia Museum of Fine Art, Columbia, South Carolina. "The Ascendancy of American Painting"

Amon Carter Museum of Western Art, Fort Worth, Texas. "Selections from Fort Worth Collections"

Tate Gallery, London. "American Painting"

University of Oregon, Eugene. "Pacific Northwest Art: The Haseltine Collection"

1964

City Art Museum, St. Louis. "200 Years of American Painting"

Downtown Gallery, New York. "Modern American Drawing"

J. L. Hudson Gallery, Detroit. "W. R. Valentiner Memorial Exhibition"

1965

University of Michigan Museum of Art, Ann Arbor. "100 Contemporary American Drawings"

1966

*University of Oregon, Eugene. Retrospective exhibition

*Humboldt State College Art Gallery, Arcata, California

Phillips Collection, Washington, D.C. "Birds in Contemporary Art"

The Museum of Modern Art, New York. "The Object Transformed"

Flint Institute of Arts, Flint, Michigan. "The First Flint Invitational Exhibition of Contemporary Painting and Sculpture"

White Art Museum, Cornell University, Ithaca, New York. "The Collection of Dr. and Mrs. Milton Lurie Kramer"

1967

Waddington Galleries, London. "Works on Paper"

1968

Dayton Art Institute, Dayton, Ohio. "A Contemporary Selection"

Herron Museum of Art, Indianapolis. "Painting and Sculpture Today"

1969

Krannert Art Museum, University of Illinois, Champaign-Urbana. "American Paintings and Sculpture"

Worcester Art Museum, Worcester, Massachusetts. "Art in America—Paintings, Drawings, Prints, and Sculpture from the Museum's Collection"

1971

*Tacoma Museum of Art. Retrospective exhibition

Minnesota Museum of Art, St. Paul. "Drawings U.S.A./71"

Lerner-Misrachi Gallery, New York. "Inner Spaces, Outer Limits: Myths and Mythmakers"

1972

Minnesota Museum of Art, St. Paul. "Drawings in St. Paul"

A.C.A. Galleries, New York. "Looking West"

1973

Albrecht Gallery, Museum of Art, St. Joseph, Missouri. "Drawing America 1973" (national invitational exhibition of American master draughtsmen)

Louise E. Thorne Memorial Art Gallery, Keene State College, Keene, New Hampshire. "After Audubon in Art"

1974

National Academy of Design, New York. "149th Annual Exhibition"

SELECTED BIBLIOGRAPHY

Although there have been some fine exhibition catalogues and many magazine and newspaper articles about Morris Graves' exhibited works, this is the first book devoted to Graves. We would like to call the reader's attention, however, to the following outstanding exhibition catalogues, articles, and books.

EXHIBITION CATALOGUES

Morris Graves. Catalogue of the retrospective exhibition organized and shown in 1956 by the Art Galleries of the University of California at Los Angeles and shown thereafter at the following institutions: Whitney Museum of American Art, New York; Phillips Collection, Washington, D.C.; Museum of Fine Arts, Boston; Des Moines Art Center; M. H. de Young Memorial Museum, San Francisco; La Jolla Museum of Art, La Jolla, California; Seattle Art Museum. Foreword by John I. H. Baur; "About the Technic," by Duncan Phillips; text by Frederick S. Wight. University of California Press, Berkeley and Los Angeles, 1956.

Morris Graves: A Retrospective. Catalogue of an exhibition held at the University of Oregon Museum of Art, Eugene, Oregon, 1966. Foreword by Wallace S. Baldinger; "Something About Morris Graves," by Virginia Haseltine; "Prophetic Speculations on the Artist's Symbolism," by Gerald Heard; "Three Kinds of Space," by Morris Graves. University of Oregon, Eugene, 1966.

ARTICLES

Valentiner, W. R., "Morris Graves." *Art Quarterly,* Number VII, 4, Autumn 1944, pp. 250–56.

Rexroth, Kenneth, "The Visionary Painting of Morris Graves." *Perspectives USA,* Number 10, Winter 1955, pp. 58–66.

Cohen, George Michael, "The Bird Paintings of Morris Graves." *College Art Journal,* Number XVIII, 1, Fall 1958, pp. 2–19.

BOOKS

Soby, James Thrall, *Contemporary Painters.* New York, The Museum of Modern Art, 1948, pp. 40–50.

Rodman, Selden, *Conversations with Artists* (introduction by Alexander Eliot). New York, Devin-Adair, 1957, pp. 6–14.

Kuh, Katharine, *The Artist's Voice.* New York and Evanston, Harper & Row, 1962, pp. 105–117.

WORKS IN PUBLIC COLLECTIONS, U.S.A.

Works by Morris Graves are also in public collections in Canada, South America, and Europe.

ARIZONA

Museum of Art, University of Arizona, Tucson

CALIFORNIA

Bank of America, Los Angeles
Art Gallery, University of California at Los Angeles
Pasadena Art Museum
San Francisco Museum of Art
Santa Barbara Museum of Art

COLORADO

Denver Art Museum

CONNECTICUT

Wadsworth Atheneum, Hartford

DELAWARE

Delaware Art Museum, Wilmington

DISTRICT OF COLUMBIA

United States Department of Labor
The Phillips Collection
Joseph H. Hirshhorn Museum and Sculpture Garden, Smith-
    sonian Institution
Woodward Foundation

GEORGIA

Atlanta Art Alliance

ILLINOIS

Art Collection, University of Illinois, Champaign-Urbana
The Arts Club of Chicago
Art Institute of Chicago

INDIANA

Fort Wayne Museum of Art

MAINE

Museum of Art, Ogunquit

MARYLAND

Baltimore Museum of Art

MASSACHUSETTS

Boston Museum of Fine Arts
Fogg Art Museum, Cambridge
William H. Lane Foundation, Leominster
Worcester Art Museum

MICHIGAN

Detroit Institute of Arts
Upjohn Company, Kalamazoo

MINNESOTA

Walker Art Center, Minneapolis
Minnesota Museum of Art, St. Paul

MISSOURI

City Art Museum of St. Louis

NEBRASKA

University of Nebraska Art Galleries, Lincoln
Joslyn Museum, Omaha

NEW YORK

Albright-Knox Art Gallery, Buffalo
Guggenheim Museum, New York
Memorial Sloan-Kettering Cancer Center, New York
The Metropolitan Museum of Art, New York
The Museum of Modern Art, New York
National Institute of Arts and Letters, New York
Sara Roby Foundation, New York
Whitney Museum of American Art, New York
Roy R. Neuberger Museum of Art, The State University of
    New York. College at Purchase
Munson-Williams-Proctor Institute, Utica

NORTH CAROLINA

North Carolina Museum of Art, Raleigh

OHIO

Cleveland Museum of Art
Columbus Gallery of Fine Art
Dayton Art Institute

OREGON

Museum of Art, University of Oregon, Eugene
Portland Art Museum

PENNSYLVANIA

Philadelphia Museum of Art

TEXAS

The Michener Collection, University of Texas, Austin
Dallas Museum of Fine Arts
Amon Carter Museum, Fort Worth
Fort Worth Art Center-Museum

VIRGINIA

Randolph-Macon Woman's College, Lynchburg

WASHINGTON

Seattle Art Museum
Henry Gallery, University of Washington, Seattle
Pacific National Bank of Washington, Seattle
Tacoma Art Museum

WISCONSIN

Milwaukee Art Center
Johnson Collection, Racine